American
English in Mind

Herbert Puchta & Jeff Stranks
with Richard Carter & Peter Lewis-Jones

Workbook **3**

CAMBRIDGE
UNIVERSITY PRESS

CAMBRIDGE
UNIVERSITY PRESS

32 Avenue of the Americas, New York, NY 10013-2473, USA

Cambridge University Press is part of the University of Cambridge.

It furthers the University's mission by disseminating knowledge in the pursuit of education, learning and research at the highest international levels of excellence.

www.cambridge.org
Information on this title: www.cambridge.org/9780521733601

© Cambridge University Press 2011

First published 2011
7th printing 2015

Printed in Mexico by Editorial Impresora Apolo, S.A. de C.V.

A catalogue record for this publication is available from the British Library

ISBN 978-0-521-73354-0 Student's Book 3
ISBN 978-0-521-73355-7 Combo 3A
ISBN 978-0-521-73356-4 Combo 3B
ISBN 978-0-521-73360-1 Workbook 3
ISBN 978-0-521-73361-8 Teacher's Edition 3
ISBN 978-0-521-73362-5 Class Audio 3
ISBN 978-0-521-73336-6 Classware 3
ISBN 978-0-521-73363-2 Testmaker 3
ISBN 978-0-521-73369-4 DVD 3

Art direction, book design and layout: Pentacor plc
Photo research: Copyright Works Inc.

Contents

1 What can we do?

1 Grammar review

✱ Simple present vs. present continuous

a Complete the sentences. Use the simple present or present continuous form of the verbs.

I'm Christy Bell, and I'm in 11th grade at a school in Chicago. This year I have to take the ACT test, so I ___don't have___ (not have) as much free time as I did before. When I [1]_____ (not do) my homework or studying for tests, I try to see my friends. Saturday night is really the only time when everyone's free because most of my friends [2]_____ (work) on Saturdays. I have a job in a home-and-garden store, but now it [3]_____ (get) harder to find enough time to work and do all of my homework, too. I [4]_____ (need) the money though because I don't get any allowance from my parents. I [5]_____ (babysit), which is good because I usually [6]_____ (get) my homework done at the same time, and I get paid for it!

Most of my classmates seem to spend a lot of their free time on computers. More and more of them [7]_____ (get) computer games or playing games online, but I don't like that very much. And these days, people [8]_____ (use) instant messaging to communicate with friends, but I [9]_____ (prefer) texting my friends on my cell phone. I hate sitting in front of a computer for hours. I do enough of that with my homework!

b Circle the correct words.

Liz: Hi, John. How [1]*you are / are you* doing?

John: I'm great. Thanks.

Liz: What [2]*do you do / are you doing* right now?

John: [3]*I look / I'm looking* at this website about global warming.

Liz: Really? [4]*Are you / Are you being* interested in the environment?

John: Yes, I am. [5]*I take / I'm taking* Mr. Ellison's environmental science class.

Liz: [6]*I don't have / I'm not having* that class this semester. [7]*Is it / Is it being* good?

John: Yes, it is. [8]*I learn / I'm learning* a lot!

Liz: Maybe I should take it next semester.

John: You should. Hey, what [9]*do you do / are you doing* right now?

Liz: Not much. Why?

John: Well, there's a march for global warming next week. [10]*I make / I'm making* some flyers for the event. [11]*I need / I'm needing* to finish them today. Do you want to help me?

Liz: Well, [12]*I babysit / I'm babysitting* my sister, but I can come in about an hour.

John: Great! See you then.

✱ Tag questions

c Match the parts of the sentences.

1 He's never on time,	_d_	a isn't she?
2 She's going to the march,	....	b didn't you?
3 They didn't come to the event,	....	c can we?
4 You recycled those newspapers,	....	d is he?
5 We can't drive here,	....	e should you?
6 Jake and Luke can take that class,	....	f did they?
7 Mrs. Park should be there,	....	g shouldn't she?
8 You shouldn't recycle the battery,	....	h can't they?

d Complete each tag question. Write one word in each blank.

1 He's just a child, *isn't* he?

2 It isn't easy being a teenager, _____ it?

3 They're only two years old. They're toddlers, _____ they?

4 Leaving the faucet on wastes water, _____ it?

5 You recycled that paper, _____ you?

6 We can't go on destroying rain forests, _____ we?

7 Your sister has just had a baby, _____ she?

8 We shouldn't litter on the street, _____ we?

9 The atmosphere has gotten very polluted, _____ it?

10 One day you'll be a pilot, _____ you?

✱ Ways of talking about the future

e Read the sentences. Mark them *A* if it is an arrangement, *P* if it is a prediction or *I* if it is an intention.

1 "I've decided on a subject to <u>study</u> in college – biology." | *I* |

2 "<u>We've</u> arranged to <u>visit</u> my grandparents on Saturday." | |

3 "<u>My dad</u>? <u>Give</u> me money to buy a new computer? Definitely not!" | |

4 "I called the doctor and made an appointment to <u>see</u> her tomorrow morning." | |

5 "<u>Planes fly</u> from England to Australia in 10 hours in the future? Yes, definitely." | |

6 "<u>My friend Mike</u> has decided to <u>leave</u> college next year." | |

f Use the <u>underlined</u> words in Exercise 1e to make sentences. For arrangements, use the present continuous; for predictions, use *will/won't*; for intentions, use *going to*.

1 *I'm going to study biology in college.* _____

2 _____

3 _____

4 _____

5 _____

6 _____

✱ Verb + -*ing* vs. infinitive

9 Write words with the cues. Use the simple present and verb + -*ing* or verb + infinitive.

1 Joe / want / study / Portuguese

Joe wants to study Portuguese. _____

2 I / not mind / recycle / every day

_____

3 Kendra / enjoy / attend / marches

_____

4 Marcos and Lee / promise / help / me with my homework

_____

5 Martin / never / offer / do / the dishes

_____

6 Penny / not stand / take / the bus to school

_____

2 Pronunciation

✱ Unstressed *to*

▶ **CD3 T16** Listen and repeat. Pay particular attention to the <u>underlined</u> words.

1 Ted didn't want <u>to</u> go shopping.

2 Mia offered <u>to</u> drive me home.

3 We decided <u>to</u> go camping for vacation.

4 Did you learn <u>to</u> play your guitar yet?

3 Vocabulary

✱ Describing someone's age and the environment

seniorcitizenwastechildtoddlerforestfumesbabylitteratmosphereteenageryoungadultpollution

a Find 11 more words or phrases in the wordsnake. Write them in the correct columns.

Age	Environment
senior citizen	

b Label the pictures with the correct phrases in the box.

> drop litter   keep buildings clean   pick up trash
> waste water

Help Out!

Here are some easy ways you can help the environment.

① Don't .... in the street.

② .... in your neighborhood.

③ Don't ....
Turn the faucet off when you're not using it.

④ Take care of public places. For example, help ....

✱ Medicine and health

c Circle the correct words.

1 He fell down outside and broke his leg. An *ambulance* / *shot* took him to the hospital.

2 I went to the doctor, and she gave me *a surgeon* / *a shot*.

3 If you carry that heavy bag, you might *hurt* / *pain* yourself.

4 I hit my arm this morning, and now it's really *hurt* / *sore*.

5 Thousands of people are sick. It's *an epidemic* / *a cold*.

6 She has a headache and a very high *temperature* / *pain*.

7 My uncle had to see the doctor because of the *sore* / *pain* in his back.

8 Some doctors complain that they have too many *shots* / *patients*.

4 Fiction in mind

a Read more of *Staying Together*. Ikuko has arrived in England. How does she feel when she first arrives? How do you think she feels after her first day at the language center?

Ikuko carried the suitcase into her room. Now she could take a shower and change her clothes. But first she must call Hiroshi. She got her cell phone out of her bag and dialed his number.

5 "So what's Birmingham like?" he asked, sounding very far away. He'd never understood why she'd wanted to study in Birmingham.

And now she wasn't so sure. She walked over to the window of her small bedroom and looked
10 out. Everything looked cold and dark in the early morning light.

"Well," she said, "it's sort of gray."

An hour later, Ikuko found the dining room of the hostel. She walked in shyly. She looked around
15 and saw that quite a few people were sitting alone. "Maybe I'm not the only person who's just arrived," she thought.

As she sat alone eating, Ikuko wondered if any of the students in the room were English. She could
20 see a group of Japanese students – a boy with bright yellow hair and two girls dressed in fashionable clothes. Nearer to her was a group of girls talking in English and another language. Everyone looked very young.

25 "Will I have anything in common with these people?" she thought. "Maybe I should just get a flight back to Japan."

Ten minutes later, she walked out into the street. She took out a map she'd been given with directions
30 to the language center and started to walk. She was supposed to get a bus, but where was the bus stop? She tried to figure it out from her map.

Then someone spoke to her in Japanese. "Are you going to the language center?"

35 She turned around. It was the Japanese boy with the yellow hair. He was with two other students.

"Yes . . . yes," she said to the Japanese boy. "On the 65 bus?"

"That's right." Then he continued in English. "Come with us. We're all going, too."

40 And when they were sitting in a club that evening, Ikuko realized that she already had friends.

b Read the text again. Mark the sentences *T* (true) or *F* (false). Correct the false statements.

before
1 Ikuko calls Hiroshi ~~after~~ she takes a shower. ....F....

2 The weather isn't very nice in England. ....

3 Ikuko ate with a group of people. ....

4 Ikuko thinks about going back to Japan. ....

5 Ikuko takes the 65 bus to the hostel. ....

6 Ikuko goes to a club with new friends after class. ....

Judith Wilson

Staying Together

CAMBRIDGE
UNIVERSITY PRESS

⑤ Write

a Read Josh's essay about going to a presentation. Write the paragraph numbers next to the topics.

.... what he learned

.... background information

.... connecting with people

1 I never knew how much I was hurting the environment until I went to a presentation by an environmentalist at a bookstore last week. I knew that people were polluting the environment, but I thought the problem was so big that there was nothing I could do. I was wrong!

2 I learned that there are a few easy things I can do to help. For example, I can turn off the faucet when I'm not using the water. Before, I would let the water run while I was brushing my teeth. Now I turn the faucet off, and then I turn it back on when I'm done brushing.

3 There were two students from my school at the presentation. We decided to try to get the school to start recycling. I also met some kids from other schools, and we're going to email each other! It was a great experience, and I hope I can make a small difference now.

b Read the essay again. Answer the questions.

1 Why did Josh think he couldn't help the environment?

2 What is one way Josh is helping the environment now?

3 What does Josh plan to do at his school?

c Write an essay about something you did this month. Write your essay in 120–150 words.

WRITING TIP

Writing about personal experiences

- Choose what you want to write about carefully. If it is for an assignment, make sure your personal experience fits the assignment. For example, if you are asked to write about an important memory, choose something from the past, not something you want to do in the future. If the topic is left open, write about something that is important or interesting to you.

- Only write about what really happened. Writing about a personal experience is not a story. You must write about what happened to you.

- Don't write harmful things about other people. If you have strong opinions about someone, it would be best not to include that information or not use the person's name.

- You do not need to include every detail about what happened. Think about the experience and include only the important and interesting details.

- Organize what you write. Use different paragraphs for different aspects of the experience. For example, what happened first, second and third. Or what you did, what you felt, how it changed you.

Unit check

1 Fill in the blanks

Complete the text with the words in the box.

> are going to start   ~~are wasting~~   is going to call   isn't it   making   recycle
> teenagers   to start   trash   will start

We _are wasting_ a lot of paper at my school, so my friends and I ¹_____ a program to ²_____ paper. I went to an environmental presentation last week. I learned that it's easy for ³_____ to get involved! We want ⁴_____ the program soon. I can't stand ⁵_____ phone calls, so my friend Tim ⁶_____ the local recycling center. We ⁷_____ the program in a month. We need to teach students what to recycle and what is ⁸_____ . We think it's going to be successful. It's a great idea, ⁹_____ ?

☐ 9

2 Choose the correct answers

(Circle) the correct answer: a, b or c.

1 Hi, Olivia. Where _____ you?

   a being   b is   c (are)

2 Hey, Paulo. What _____ right now?

   a are you doing   b do you do   c does you do

3 We should recycle more, _____ we?

   a should   b shouldn't   c wouldn't

4 Don didn't attend the march, _____ ?

   a does he   b didn't he   c did he

5 I promise _____ my room today.

   a to clean   b cleaning   c clean

6 I don't mind _____ for you.

   a to wait   b waiting   c wait

7 My brother _____ me at 6:00.

   a to meet   b is meeting   c are meeting

8 We're _____ a recycling program.

   a going to start   b going to   c go to starting

9 It _____ rain tomorrow for our soccer game.

   a not going to   b not willing   c won't

☐ 8

3 Vocabulary

Underline the word that doesn't fit in each group.

1 ambulance	surgeon	<u>toddler</u>	epidemic
2 pollution	clean	trash	litter
3 sore	drop	pain	hurt
4 cold	temperature	epidemic	recycle
5 forest	teenager	adult	baby
6 waste	fumes	sore	pollution
7 drop	pick up	recycle	epidemic
8 child	adult	ambulance	senior citizen
9 shot	pick up	patient	pain

☐ 8

How did you do?

Total: ☐ 25

🙂 Very good 25 – 20	😐 OK 19 – 16	🙁 Review Unit 1 again 15 or less

2 Making choices

1 Grammar review

✱ Present perfect with *for* or *since*

a Complete the sentences with *for* or *since*.

1 Jiro has been in Boston __*since*__ the beginning of the summer.

2 He has studied English _____ he was seven years old.

3 His mother has been with him in Boston _____ two weeks.

4 He hasn't eaten any hamburgers _____ he arrived.

5 He hasn't had any good sushi _____ he left Tokyo.

6 He hasn't seen his friends _____ a long time.

b Make sentences with the present perfect of the underlined verb and *for* or *since*.

1 I <u>have</u> a bicycle. My parents gave it to me last year. _*I've had my bicycle for a year / since last year.*_

2 I'<u>m</u> in this class. I started the class six months ago. _____

3 Joanna and I <u>are</u> friends. We became friends in 2009. _____

4 I <u>know</u> Paul Carpenter. I met him a year ago. _____

✱ Comparatives and superlatives

c Look at the chart. 1 = the most, 3 = the least. Write sentences about the places with the words in parentheses.

City in Texas:	Dallas	Houston	Austin
big	2	1	3
clean	2	3	1
dangerous	1	2	3
busy	2	1	3
exciting	3	2	1

1 (big / city) _Houston is the biggest city._

2 (Dallas / Austin / big) _Dallas is bigger than Austin._

3 (clean / city) _____

4 (Houston / Austin / dangerous) _____

5 (dangerous / city) _____

6 (busy / city) _____

7 (Dallas / Houston / exciting) _____

8 (exciting / city) _____

✱ used to

d Look at the information about people who have changed things in their lives. Write sentences.

Name	In the past	Now
Peter	meat	fish
Sandra	tea	coffee
Amanda	dog	cat
Julia	magazines	newspapers
Hiro	car	bicycle
Daniel	TV	sports

(eat)   1   *Peter used to eat meat, but now he eats fish.*

(drink)   2   ....

(have)   3   ....

(read)   4   ....

(drive/ride)   5   ....

(watch/play)   6   ....

✱ must not vs. don't have

e Circle the correct words.

1   You *don't have to* / *must not* drive fast. We have a lot of time.

2   You *don't have to* / *must not* drive fast. This road is full of holes and is very dangerous.

3   You *don't have to* / *must not* buy a new laptop. They're too expensive.

4   You *don't have to* / *must not* buy a new laptop. I can fix your old one easily.

5   You *don't have to* / *must not* tell Sarah about the party. I invited her last night.

6   You *don't have to* / *must not* tell Lucas about the party. I really don't want him to know about it.

7   You *don't have to* / *must not* get up early today. It's a holiday.

8   You *don't have to* / *must not* get up early today. The doctor told you to stay in bed.

9   You *don't have to* / *must not* wash my new dress. It can only be dry-cleaned.

10 You *don't have to* / *must not* wash my new dress. It isn't dirty.

2 Pronunciation

✱ Intonation in questions with *or*

▶ CD3 T17   Write a line going down where the intonation goes down.
Write a line going up where the intonation goes up. Then listen and repeat.

1   Are you going to go to Orlando or Miami?

2   Is he eating a taco or a hot dog?

3   Did he say *pants* or *dance*?

4   Do you have a brother or a sister?

5   Have you known her for one year or two years?

6   Do they live in an apartment or a house?

3 Vocabulary

✱ American vs. British English

a Sally is a British teenager. She's writing to her new American e-pal, Mina. Find eight words (one on each line) that Mina might not understand. Change them to American English.

Hi Mina!

My name is Sally, and I'm going to tell you about myself. I live in London. Our flat ⟶ _apartment_

is on the 10th floor, so we have to go up in a lift to get to it! The place where we live ⟶ _____

is OK, but unfortunately, a lot of people around here throw rubbish in the street instead ⟶ _____

of throwing it away, so the pavements get dirty. That's not really nice, is it? Anyway, ⟶ _____

what else can I tell you? Well, I like football a lot, but I don't play it. I just watch ⟶ _____

it on TV. I think perhaps I should get some exercise because I eat a lot! I just love biscuits, ⟶ _____

and most days I eat a lot of sweets, too. I'm not the healthiest person in the world! ⟶ _____

Starting next week, though, I'm going to start walking to school (now I use the underground), ⟶ _____

so that will help me be healthier, I hope!

Write soon and tell me about yourself, OK? Bye!

✱ Homes

b Match the words with their definitions. Write a–f in the boxes.

1 floor	**c**	a something put up around a yard to protect it
2 garage	☐	b steps going from one level to another
3 yard	☐	c a level of a building, like first, second, third
4 apartment	☐	d a place to keep cars
5 fence	☐	e an area near a house with grass, trees and flowers
6 stairs	☐	f a set of rooms to live in within a large building

✱ Information technology

c Complete the crossword puzzle.

1 I bought a power _____cord_____ for my laptop.

2 My computer has two CD _____ .

3 _____ the video from the Internet. It's free.

4 Dad installed a Wi-Fi _____ at home.

5 Log _____ to access this site.

6 I can't type! My _____ is broken.

7 Do you use a mouse or a touch _____ ?

8 I remember my user name, but I can't remember my _____ .

9 How many USB _____ does this computer have?

✱ Noun suffixes

d | Write the words from the box with their suffixes in the correct place in the chart.

~~cancel~~ entertain equip explain improve journal
reception reserve

-ation	-ist	-ment
cancellation		

4 Listen

Use the words from "Born to Try" to complete the sentences. Check with the song on page 12 of the Student Book.

fate protect ~~regret~~ remove sacrifice

1 **Marcos:** Hey, Wendy, did you talk to Rita?

   Wendy: Yes, she's upset about what you said.

   Marcos: I know. I really ___regret___ saying it. I'm going to call her and apologize right now.

2 **Doug:** This jacket is really stylish, but it's expensive!

   Peter: Sometimes you have to _____ style for price.

   Doug: I know. I guess I'll get the plain black one. It's a lot cheaper.

3 **Cindy:** Did you meet my friend Lee last night?

   Maria: Yes, I think it was _____ . We were meant to be friends. He's so nice, and he likes photography, like me!

4 **Hiro:** I can't get this pen to work.

   Tina: You didn't _____ the top!

   Hiro: Oh, yeah. Thanks.

5 **Jenny:** Can you go to the concert on Friday?

   Jill: No, my parents said it was too late.

   Jenny: Really? That's too bad.

   Jill: I know they're just trying to _____ me, but it's really annoying!

5 Study help

✱ Prioritizing

It's important to *prioritize* your time when you study. In other words, do the most important things first. Here are some tips on how to prioritize your time.

1 Make a list of everything you have to do for the week for class.

2 Look at your list and put the most important things first. What is due first? Which test is the hardest? Rewrite your list in the order of importance.

3 Each night, look at your list. Do the most important things first. Cross off the items you finish.

4 Change your list as you need to. You might get a new homework assignment. Decide where it should go on your list and rearrange your schedule.

Skills in mind

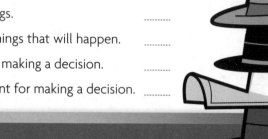

6 Read

Read the article. Then answer the questions. Mark *T* (true) or *F* (false).

1 The Six Thinking Hats strategy helps you make decisions. ___*T*___

2 With the White Hat, think about your feelings. _____

3 With the Yellow Hat, think about positive things that will happen. _____

4 Never think of other possible choices when making a decision. _____

5 In the end, the Red Hat is the most important for making a decision. _____

The Six Thinking Hats

Everyone has important decisions to make in life. Often there are many possible choices. The Six Thinking Hats is a strategy that helps you make decisions. "Put" each colored hat on and think about the decision you have to make.

The White Hat
Think about the facts. What information do you have? What information do you need? How can you get it? Learn everything you need to know about something before you make a decision.

The Red Hat
Think about your emotions. How will this decision make you feel? How will it make close friends and family feel?

The Yellow Hat
Think about all of the benefits that will come from your decision. What good will come from your choice? What other opportunities will come up after you make the decision?

The Black Hat
Think about all of the negative things that could happen once you make your decision. Could anything bad happen? What risks are there?

The Green Hat
Think creatively. Are there alternatives to your original choice? What else could you do?

The Blue Hat
Keep things in control. Put the Blue Hat on and access what you thought about with the other five hats. And then come to a decision!

READING TIP

How to answer true/false questions

You will have to answer many true/false questions for homework and for tests. There are strategies you can use to help you do well on true/false questions.

- Read the questions before you read the text. Think about what the answers might be.

- Read the entire text. Do not stop to answer questions.

- Go back to the questions. Answer the ones you can.

- Read the text again, focusing on the questions.

- Look for key words in the reading that are also in the questions.

- Sometimes true/false questions do not use the same words as the text. Look for synonyms in the reading for words in the questions.

- Negatives can be confusing in true/false questions. Read sentences with *no, not, don't, never* and other negatives carefully.

- Remember, if part of the statement is false, the entire item is false (even if part of the statement is true!).

Unit check

1 Fill in the blanks

Complete the text with the words in the box.

biscuit for journalist more difficult reservation ~~since~~ soccer than the best used to

Hi, I'm Yolanda. I've been studying English ___*since*___ 1999. I ¹_____ take classes at the Filmore Language School, but now I study English at my university. I studied in Vancouver, Canada, ²_____ two years. It was ³_____ way to learn English. I also spent a summer in London. It was ⁴_____ to understand English in London ⁵_____ it was in Vancouver. There were many words I didn't know. For example, in British English they say ⁶_____ instead of cookie. And they say football instead of ⁷_____ . It was a little confusing! I made friends in both places. Next week, I'm going to Vancouver for a week to visit my friend Kayla. She's a ⁸_____ , and she works for a newspaper. I have a ⁹_____ at a beautiful hotel near her apartment!

	9

2 Choose the correct answers

(Circle) the correct answer: a, b or c.

1 Costa Rica is _____ Mexico.
   a small   b (smaller than)   c the smallest

2 Tokyo is _____ city I've visited.
   a more beautiful   b more beautiful than
   c the most beautiful

3 I _____ drive to work, but now I walk.
   a use   b use to   c used to

4 You _____ call me. I'll be in the library, and I can't talk on the phone.
   a have to   b must not   c don't have to

5 You _____ take me to the airport. John is taking me.
   a have to   b must not   c don't have to

6 Pedro is _____ his older brother.
   a as tall   b as tall as   c tall as

7 I've been studying English _____ six years.
   a for   b since   c to

8 She's known Jane _____ 1993.
   a for   b since   c to

9 This is _____ vacation ever!
   a good   b better   c the best

	8

3 Vocabulary

Put the words in the correct place in the chart.

download   garage   keyboard   ~~lift~~   lorry   memory stick   mobile home   rubbish   network stairs   trousers   yard

British English	Information technology	Homes
lift		

	11

How did you do?

Total: | 28 |

☺	Very good 28 – 22	☺	OK 21 – 16	☹	Review Unit 2 again 15 or less

3 Communication

1 Grammar

⭐ Simple past vs. present perfect

a Complete the dialogues. Use the simple past or the present perfect form of the verbs in parentheses.

1 **Andy:** _____*Have*_____ you two _____*met*_____ (meet) before?

  Lauren: Yes. We both _____*went*_____ (go) to that party last week.

2 **Setsuko:** How long _____ you _____ (know) Mark?

  Andres: We _____ (meet) on the first day of this class.

3 **Terrance:** _____ you _____ (see) any movies last weekend?

  Shayla: No. I _____ (not go) to the movies for ages.

4 **Ramon:** _____ you _____ (finish) that Harry Potter book yet?

  Tessa: Oh, yes, I _____ (take) it back to the library yesterday.

5 **Jay:** _____ you _____ (speak) to Will yesterday?

  Maya: No, I _____ (not see) him for a couple of days.

6 **Carrie:** _____ you _____ (buy) Lee's birthday present yet?

  Jen: Yes, I _____ (get) her something in town last night.

7 **Shandra:** When _____ you _____ (learn) to drive?

  Jack: Me? I _____ (never drive) a car in my life.

b Complete the questions. Use the simple past or present perfect.

1 **A:** I have really bad toothache.

  B: Oh, I'm sorry. How long *have you had it* ?

2 **A:** We don't live on Elm Street anymore.

  B: Oh, I didn't know that. When _____ ?

3 **A:** We had a great time at the movies last night.

  B: Oh, really? What movie _____ ?

4 **A:** I lived in Japan when I was younger.

  B: That's interesting. How long _____ there?

5 **A:** I'm working part-time in a restaurant.

  B: Oh, yeah? When _____ ?

6 **A:** So, you finally arrived!

  B: Sorry I'm late! How long _____ here?

c Complete the sentences with the simple present, simple past and present perfect forms of the verbs in parentheses.

1 I _____*know*_____ Pete. I _____ him for years. In fact, our grandfathers _____ each other when they were alive. (know)

2 He _____ at this restaurant since last summer. He _____ in the kitchen. Before that, he _____ in a store. (work)

3 When she was younger, she _____ in Russia. Now she _____ in Japan. She _____ there for five years. (live)

4 I _____ my leg. I _____ it on a skiing trip last month. I _____ something every time I ski. (break)

d Read the diary of a woman who went to a seminar to learn how to talk to animals. Some of the lines have a word that should not be there. Write the word at the end of the line, or check (✔) if the line is correct.

I arrived here last night. Today we all paid our fee, $160 for an eight-hour	1 ✔
workshop. Then we got to know our trainer, a woman ~~is~~ named Clara.	2 *is*
"I've had have horses since my childhood," she said. "But it took me a	3
long while to find out that I can understand them! You can to learn this, too.	4
Animals talk all the time. You just need to learn to listen to them." After	5
breakfast we have worked in pairs. "Close your eyes, think of a message	6
and communicate it through your thoughts," Clara said. I decided	7
to "tell" to my partner that "The mountain is purple." After two minutes of	8
concentration (I got a headache), she told for me what she understood: "It's	9
too hot in here!" Well, never mind, we're here to read the thoughts of	10
animals, not humans! After lunch, we did sat on the grass near Clara's	11
horses and closed our eyes. Half an hour since later, we went back to the	12
house. So what messages did we have read? "It's hot." "We like the grass."	13
Do I really need an animal communicator to learn that a horses like grass?	14

✱ Time expressions

e Two time expressions are correct, and one is incorrect. ~~Cross out~~ the incorrect answer.

1 Have you called your mother *already / yet / ~~yesterday~~*?
2 Philip *already / just / in 2004* left school.
3 We didn't have time to clean up *last night / already / before we left*.
4 Actually, I saw that movie *two days ago / just / on Sunday*.
5 They've haven't seen snow *last winter / yet / since they moved*.
6 I haven't heard from Mike *since the party / for a few days / about a week ago*.
7 We had an old black car *when I was little / since the 80s / for about ten years*.

f Rewrite the sentences using the words in parentheses.

1 I've known Mrs. Taylor for four years. (met)
   I met Mrs. Taylor four years ago.
2 Jessica bought her cell phone last week. (for)

3 William called a minute ago. (just)

4 How long have you had that bag? (buy)

5 Your friends have been here for an hour. (ago)

6 Your birthday cards got here yesterday. (since)

7 The last time I saw you was at your party. (haven't)

2 Pronunciation

✱ Sentence stress

a Read the sentences. <u>Underline</u> the words that are stressed. Sometimes there is more than one possibility.

1 How long have you had it?
2 When did you move?
3 What book did you read?
4 How long did you live there?
5 When did you start working there?
6 How long have you been here?

b ▶ CD3 T18 Listen, check and repeat.

3 Vocabulary

✱ Body language

a Match the two parts of the sentences. Write a–j in the boxes.

1	That guy's leaning	*i*	a	back in your chair and enjoy the concert.
2	Could you try to make		b	you that warm smile when you walk in the room.
3	Just sit		c	your eyebrows at me? Is there a problem?
4	If you agree, nod		d	nervous, even if you feel it!
5	Just try to avoid		e	eye contact with the waiter? I need some water.
6	She's fantastic. She always gives		f	eye contact if you don't want to talk to him.
7	Try not to look		g	about? Do you think she's in trouble?
8	Did you just raise		h	your arms. I hope you're not getting impatient with me.
9	I see you've just folded		i	forward a lot. Do you think he's trying to listen to us?
10	What do you think she's gesturing		j	your head three times.

✱ *say* and *tell*

b Complete the sentences with the correct form of *say* or *tell*.

1 I can't _____tell_____ the difference between the new version and the old one.

2 If something is bothering you, please _____ it out loud. Don't whisper to your friends.

3 He's only two years old, but he can already _____ the time.

4 Can I _____ you a secret if you promise to keep it to yourself?

5 I hope you're not _____ me a lie. You'll be in trouble if you are.

6 I'm sure you've _____ me that joke before. Don't you know any others?

c Complete the sentences with the correct form of *say* or *tell* and one of the expressions in the box.

> thank you   sorry   goodbye   ~~please~~   off his boss   him a story   the truth   that again

1 If you want something, you really should _____*say please*_____ .

2 Ouch! That really hurt! Aren't you going to _____ ?

3 Sorry, I didn't hear you. Could you _____ ?

4 I don't believe you! Are you sure you're _____ ?

5 That's a really nice present your grandma sent you. You need to write and _____ .

6 He won't go to sleep until you _____ .

7 Well, that's the end of the class. It's time to _____ .

8 Alan didn't like his job, so he _____ . Then he quit.

d **Vocabulary bank** Replace the underlined words with a phrase from the box. Write a–j in the boxes.

> a made small talk b talk back c speak a word of d on speaking terms e talk sports
> f Talk about g ~~spoke too soon~~ h Speak up i speak your mind j talking shop

1 Mom said it wasn't going to rain, but she said that <u>without thinking</u>. The sky's full of dark clouds. `g`

2 I can't hear a word you're saying. <u>Talk more loudly</u>, please. `[ ]`

3 Alex, don't <u>reply rudely</u> to the teacher like that! `[ ]`

4 I only spoke English when I was on vacation in Spain, because I can't <u>say anything at all</u> in Spanish. `[ ]`

5 I'd like you to <u>tell me exactly what you think</u>. `[ ]`

6 I don't want to go out with Tom and his friends. They just <u>discuss things like football</u> all the time. `[ ]`

7 We didn't know what to say to each other, so we just <u>talked about unimportant things</u>. `[ ]`

8 I just read this book. <u>It's absolutely fantastic</u>! You really must read it. `[ ]`

9 Dad loves <u>discussing work</u> with his colleagues. `[ ]`

10 Francesca and Ally were arguing again. They aren't <u>communicating with each other at all</u> right now. `[ ]`

4 Culture in mind

Read the text. Then mark the statements *T* (true), *F* (false) or *N* (not enough information).

1 Africans used drumming before Europeans discovered the continent. `[ ]`

2 Slaves used drumming to send messages about their slave masters. `[ ]`

3 Slave masters encouraged the use of drumming. `[ ]`

4 Some drumming sounds a little like speech. `[ ]`

5 Drumming communication differs from one country to another. `[ ]`

6 People add new words and phrases to the drumming "language" all the time. `[ ]`

7 About half of all drum messages are misunderstood. `[ ]`

Talking Drums

In some parts of Africa, drums have been used for communication for hundreds of years. That was how, for example, tribes knew that European explorers were on their way. They heard the drum messages from miles away, long before the explorers actually appeared. At one time, drums were banned, because slaves were using them to send messages to each other. The slave masters couldn't understand the messages and were worried about what the slaves were "saying," so they banned the use of the drums.

There are three types of drumming. One type uses rhythms to send a particular signal. A second type of drumming repeats the patterns of speech (i.e., it matches the rhythm of specific words or sentences). And the third type is more musical. None of the forms of drumming are official languages. Indeed, there is no international drumming language at all. Drum communication is localized and pretty limited. People can't suddenly add new expressions to the drumming, so it can't be used to say anything you want. And there is always a danger that messages will be misunderstood. Nevertheless, drumming is still a valuable way of sending limited information, where the people who hear it understand the message.

5 Write

a Read this email to Laura from her friend Nadia.

> **To:** lauranichols@aeim.cup
> **From:** n.stephens@aeim.cup
>
> Hey, girl! Just a quick email to tell you I'm still alive! Mom said I can't use my phone this month because I spent too much last month.
>
> Oh, well. Listen – email me back.
> – How's your week been?
> – Any luck with finding a job?
> – Things OK with Tom?
> – Ian Finch's party!! It's tomorrow night. Are we meeting there?
> – Any other news I should know about?
>
> Write back soon!
> Love, Nadia

b Read Laura's reply. Does she answer all of Nadia's questions? What is wrong with the underlined phrases?

c Replace the underlined phrases in Laura's reply with phrases a–f below. Write 1–6 in the boxes.

a Things are going well with Tom [3]

b So, about [ ]

c Hi Nadia, [ ]

d He's still not sure about [ ]

e Take care [ ]

f I don't really want to do that [ ]

WRITING TIP

Using appropriate language

When you write a letter or an email, it is very important to choose language that is appropriate for the reader.

- Think about who the letter is for. If it is someone you already know (a friend or an e-pal, for example), then your language can be more simple and informal.

- Make sure you include all the information you are asked to include, in a natural way.

- When you learn new words and expressions, ask your teacher if they are formal or informal. If you learn the way to start a formal letter, also find out how to start a letter to an e-pal, for example.

> **To:** n.stephens@aeim.cup
> **From:** lauranichols@aeim.cup
>
> [1]Dear Ms. Stephens,
>
> How are things? Sorry to hear about your phone problem! How are you going to survive without your cell phone? Anyway, my week's been OK – the usual stuff at college. I think I'll stay, though. I can't find any music jobs except working in the megastore at the mall, and [2]that is not a suitable option for the rest of my life.
>
> [3]My relationship with Tom is proceeding well. He's been really sweet recently. [4]He has not made a decision so far regarding going to college next year. I think he should go, even if it means we'll be apart. Decisions, decisions!
>
> [5]With reference to Ian's party – we could meet up before if you want. How about Superblast Coffee at 7:30?
>
> Guess who we bumped into today? Ben Davis! He's back from Hong Kong. He seems kind of unhappy. His parents have broken up, and he's not sure what he wants to do. He's coming to the party. You used to like Ben, didn't you?
>
> [6]Yours faithfully,
> Laura

d Write a similar 120-word email from Rebecca to Lily in which she passes on her latest news using the information from Exercise 12 on page 21 of the Student's Book.

Unit check

1 Fill in the blanks

Complete the text with the words in the box.

| back nod make ~~gesturing~~ telling eye forward warm look arms |

It's funny how different people communicate in groups. Some people are always _gesturing_ with their hands, and others just stand with their ¹_____ folded. Some talk nonstop, and others just sit ²_____ and ³_____ their heads occasionally. I have a problem with people who don't ⁴_____ eye contact. When someone doesn't look at you, it looks like they're ⁵_____ lies, especially when they ⁶_____ nervous, too. It's funny – you can give someone a ⁷_____ smile, but they still avoid ⁸_____ contact. It makes me want to lean ⁹_____ and say, "Hey, it's me, I'm talking to you!"

| 9 |

2 Choose the correct answers

Circle the correct answer: a, b or c.

1 I _____ made a terrible mistake.
   a yet   b ever   c (just)

2 She _____ seen her boyfriend all week.
   a never   b didn't   c hasn't

3 I _____ run to school in the mornings. It's only two kilometers.
   a haven't   b usually   c didn't

4 Wait! I haven't had breakfast _____ .
   a still   b ago   c yet

5 How long _____ you wait for me last night?
   a did   b have   c do

6 I can't believe you _____ off your boss and then quit.
   a say   b give   c told

7 My birthday was three days _____ .
   a ago   b just   c last

8 My brother and sister _____ bought me a present for my birthday.
   a didn't yet   b has never   c still haven't

9 You haven't _____ sorry for shouting at me.
   a say   b saying   c said

| 8 |

3 Vocabulary

Choose the correct word.

Our parents have always encouraged us to speak our ¹_minds_ . When their friends come over, they don't want us to just make small ²_____ . They ³_____ us to talk about our interests. Of course, they don't like it if we talk ⁴_____ to them. Mom tried to give my brother a ⁵_____ about that the other day, but he ⁶_____ off to his room, so he got away that time! Then I told him ⁷_____ because I didn't like the way he was talking to me, either. Mom says good manners are important. We have to say "please" and "thank you," and we have to say it out ⁸_____ so everyone hears us.

1 a words   (b) minds   c memories   d voices
2 a talk   b lies   c truth   d speak
3 a believe b reply   c tell   d notice
4 a from   b to   c at   d back
5 a sign   b warning   c telling   d saying
6 a charged b ranged   c signed   d hid
7 a in   b out   c off   d up
8 a noisy   b wide   c loud   d big

| 8 |

How did you do?

Total: | 25 |

 Very good
25 – 20

 OK
19 – 16

 Review Unit 3 again
15 or less

4 A true friend

1 Grammar

✱ Simple past vs. past continuous review

a Complete the sentences with the simple past or past continuous form of the verbs in parentheses.

1 While I _____was looking_____ (look) for my tennis balls, I _____found_____ (find) an old sandwich under my bed.

2 When my parents _____ (come) back, we _____ (have) a party.

3 When I _____ (open) the door, they _____ (dance) in the dark.

4 I _____ (find) this necklace while I _____ (clean) your room.

5 While we _____ (wait), we _____ (start) to write the invitations.

6 I _____ (teach) a gym class when I _____ (hear) about the plane crash.

7 Someone _____ (call) you on your cell phone while you _____ (take) the dog for a walk.

b Complete the sentences with the simple past or past continuous form of the verbs in parentheses.

Godzilla the cat had a special relationship with her owner, David Hart. David often _____went_____ (go) away for work. While he [1]_____ (travel), his mother [2]_____ (come) over to his house to look after the cat. One day while the telephone [3]_____ (ring), his mother [4]_____ (notice) Godzilla get up off the sofa and sit down next to the phone. She [5]_____ (pick) up the phone. It was David on the phone. The next time the phone [6]_____ (ring), Godzilla [7]_____ (do) the same thing. It was David again. But the next time, Godzilla [8]_____ (not move). His mother [9]_____ (answer) the phone. It wasn't David. She started to notice that every time David [10]_____ (call), Godzilla [11]_____ (go) to sit next to the phone. When it wasn't David, Godzilla [12]_____ (stay) where she was.

✱ Time conjunctions: *as / as soon as*

c Connect the sentences with the words in parentheses. Sometimes you need to change the order of the sentences.

1 His mother came to stay at his house. David went away to work. (when)
   When David went away to work, his mother came to stay at his house.

2 The phone started ringing. Godzilla ran and sat next to the phone. (as soon as)

   ----

3 The hall light came on. She was parking her car. (as)

   ----

4 The dog started barking. I got to the gate. (as soon as)

   ----

5 Sometimes an animal starts behaving strangely. Something happens to its owner. (when)

   ----

6 Many animals are waiting at the door. Their owners are still traveling home. (while)

   ----

2 Pronunciation

✱ Linking sounds

a Look at the way these words from Exercise 1b are linked:

her ⌣ owner   David ⌣ often
went ⌣ away   look ⌣ after

b ▶ **CD3 T19** Mark similar links in the text and then listen and check.

3 Grammar

✳ Simple past vs. past perfect

a Match the sentence halves. Write a–d in the boxes.

1 A man was arrested for a bank robbery after police called him on his cell phone. The man ...

2 A man was arrested in the hospital for trying to steal money from a house safe after police found his glove at the house. The safe ...

3 A man who had climbed Mount Everest six times died as a result of a fall at home. He ...

4 An unemployed man who tried to print his own money was caught as soon as he tried to spend it. He ...

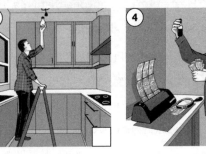

a had used black ink on the notes instead of green, because he was color-blind.

b had left a business card at the bank with his phone number on it.

c had fallen on his hand and cut off one of his fingers. The man ran away, leaving his glove behind. When the man went to the hospital with a missing finger, the police were able to match the finger to the hand.

d had climbed a ladder to change a light bulb in the kitchen when he fell and hit his head on the sink.

b Complete the sentences. Use the past perfect and the simple past or past continuous form of the verbs.

1 As soon as he ___*closed*___ (close) the door, he _____ (realize) that he _____ (leave) his key inside.

2 I _____ (have) the feeling that I _____ (meet) her somewhere before.

3 I _____ (not know) what I _____ (say) to her, but she _____ (cry).

4 They _____ (get) to the movie theater ten minutes after the movie _____ (start).

5 My cell phone _____ (not work) because I _____ (forget) to charge it.

6 I _____ (see) you sitting and smiling a half an hour before the end of the exam. _____ you already _____ (finish)?

c Read the text about the TV show *Friends*. Some of the lines have a word that should not be there. Write the incorrect extra word at the end of the line, or check (✔) if the line is correct.

Friends is still ~~being~~ one of the most popular TV shows in the world,	1	*being*
even after they stopped making it in 2004. The show had had three	2	✔
previous names before it had became simply *Friends*: *Friends Like Us*,	3	_____
Across the Hall and *Six of One*. But in the end, one word was been	4	_____
enough. Apart from the six main characters, the only other person to	5	_____
appear in all ten years that they have made the show was Gunther, the	6	_____
coffee shop server. He was having the only person in the cast that knew	7	_____
how to operate a cappuccino machine.		
Why was the show so popular? It was being usually well written and	8	_____
funny, of course, but what has kept fans watching for more than a decade	9	_____
is possibly the fact that the group of six always did stayed friends, no	10	_____
matter what were problems the characters had on screen, or the actors	11	_____
had in real life.		

4 Vocabulary

✱ Friends and enemies

a Replace the underlined words with a phrase from the box. Write a–f in the boxes.

> a let me down   b fallen out   c ~~tell on me~~   d stand by you   e get along well with
> f sticking up for me

1 Please don't <u>tell anyone that I did it</u>! I'll be your friend forever!   `c`

2 Your most loyal friends are the ones who <u>stay loyal to you</u> in the bad times.   ☐

3 Thanks for <u>supporting me</u> in there. I didn't think anyone was going to agree with me.   ☐

4 You really <u>have a good relationship with</u> your stepbrothers and stepsisters, don't you?   ☐

5 It looks like Darren and Marsha have <u>stopped being friends</u>. They don't talk to each other anymore.   ☐

6 You said you would go with me! Please don't <u>disappoint me</u>. I don't want to go alone.   ☐

b Look at the pictures. Choose a phrase from the box in Exercise 4a to complete sentences 1–5 below. There is one phrase you won't need.

1 Oh, no! What have I done? Look, don't `c` and I'll give you some of my candy.

2 It's amazing that they _____ each other.

3 Come on, computer! Please don't _____ now!

4 Phew! Thanks for _____ .

5 Oh, no! It looks like they've _____ with each other. Be careful what you say.

c **Vocabulary bank** Complete the sentences with the words in the box.

> allies   acquaintance   ~~old~~
> hit it off   friendly advice   make
> friends are for   close

1 I've known Andrew for a very long time. We're _____ old _____ friends.

2 The two countries were _____ during the war.

3 He's very shy, so it isn't easy for him to _____ friends with people.

4 We met, he liked me and I liked him. We _____ immediately!

5 They know all of each other's secrets and so on. They're really _____ friends.

6 Let me give you some _____ . You really should be nice to your sister.

7 She isn't a friend really, just a business _____ of my mother's.

8 You don't have to thank me. After all, that's what _____ .

5 Everyday English

a Complete the expressions with the words in the box.

> right   could   ~~especially~~   sooner   news   matter

1. A: Do you like Chinese food?

   B: Not ___especially___ .

2. A: You're staying after school today, _____ ?

   B: Yes, I am.

3. A: Do you mind if I copy your homework?

   B: As a _____ of fact, I do. Do it yourself.

4. A: Are you going to Diana's party?

   B: Party? That's _____ to me. I didn't know she was having one.

5. A: Mom, I'm sorry. I ate the last piece of cake.

   B: How _____ you? I was saving that for your dad.

6. A: When do you want our homework, Mr. Ito?

   B: The _____ the better, but no later than Thursday.

b Complete the dialogue with the expressions from Exercise 5a.

Steve: Hey Brian, you like MGMT, right?

Brian: [1] ___Not especially___ , why?

Steve: They're playing at The Loft in May.

Brian: Really? [2] _____ . Are you going?

Steve: Absolutely. I bought my tickets yesterday.

Brian: Tickets?

Steve: Yes, one's for Jen. I've invited her along.

Brian: What! [3] _____ ? You know I like her.

Steve: So why don't you come with us?

Brian: [4] _____ , I think I will. When should I get my ticket?

Steve: [5] _____ . They're selling really quickly.

Brian: OK, I'm going to buy mine now! See you.

THE ACADEMY PRESENTS

MGMT

IN CONCERT

MAY 12

TICKETS available

6 Study help

✱ Using formal and informal language

- When you learn new words and phrases, it is important to know if the language is formal or informal. For example, it is not appropriate to end a letter requesting information about a course with "Take care." At the same time, you can sound too formal if you write "Yours faithfully" in an email to someone you met on a school exchange program.

- Phrasal verbs are usually, but not always, more informal ways of saying something. It is fine to say to a friend "Let's meet up sometime," but in a formal situation, it would be better to say "I would like to schedule a meeting."

Skills in mind

7 Listen

▶CD3 T20 **a** Read statements A–C below, and then listen and read what the person says about pets and their owners. Decide which statement you think is the speaker's opinion.

A Pet owners have a special understanding with their animals.

B Only dogs have a telepathic relationship with their owners, not other pets.

C The special relationship between a pet and its owner does not really exist.

> "A lot of people seem to think that pets, especially dogs, are somehow telepathic. They think that they have a special understanding with their animal, so that, for example, their pet knows when they are coming home or knows when something is wrong. I think that's ridiculous, though. These things are just coincidence, or it's just that the owner is trying to wish that his or her pet is special."

The speaker says "A lot of people seem to think …," but this probably does not include the speaker. The speaker also says "especially dogs," which does not mean only dogs. The third and fourth sentences give the speaker's opinion: "I think …". The correct answer is C.

LISTENING TIP

Matching speakers with opinions

- In this kind of question, you will usually hear a number of different people talking about a similar subject.

- It is important to read the statements carefully first, to be clear about the differences between each one.

- The speakers may use different words from the ones in the statements, but the meaning will be the same.

- Try to think of other ways to express the ideas in the statements to imagine what the speaker might say. For example, when the statement is "It's not necessary," the speaker might say "You don't have to" or "You don't need to."

- The speaker may seem to be agreeing with the statement because the speaker uses the same words. However, the speaker goes on to disagree with the statement and therefore thinks the opposite. For example, the speaker might say, "*Some people* think you have to see your best friend every day, *but I don't* think that's necessary."

- Remember you are being asked for *the speaker's* opinion, not yours!

b ▶CD3 T21 Listen to five people talking about best friends, and match each speaker with one of the options A–F. Use each letter only once. There is one extra letter you won't need.

Speaker 1 ☐

Speaker 2 ☐

Speaker 3 ☐

Speaker 4 ☐

Speaker 5 ☐

A It's not necessary to see your best friend every day.

B You don't always like people the first time you meet them.

C Some people don't have any friends.

D It's not important to have a best friend.

E It's not so hard to make new best friends.

F It's normal to fight with your best friend sometimes.

Unit check

1 Fill in the blanks

Complete the text with the words in the box.

> loyalty ~~friendships~~ up out stood get letting had while friends

One of the great ___friendships___ in literature is the one between the hobbits Frodo Baggins and Samwise Gamgee in *The Lord of the Rings*. Sam, who ¹ _____ been Frodo's servant at their home in the Shire, accompanied Frodo and his company on a journey to destroy the ring and save the world. ² _____ they were making their journey, Sam ³ _____ by his master through all kinds of danger, never ⁴ _____ him down. The story shows us that, even for people who ⁵ _____ along very well, there are times when our ⁶ _____ is tested, and we can fall ⁷ _____ with each other. However, true ⁸ _____ always stick ⁹ _____ for each other in the end.

[ ] 9

2 Choose the correct answers

(Circle) the correct answer: a, b or c.

1 You're not going to tell _____ her, are you?
   a well   b down   c (on)

2 Her old car never _____ her down.
   a makes   b does   c lets

3 _____ soon as we left, the snow started.
   a While   b As   c Then

4 I _____ already bought my tickets for the show before we got to the theater.
   a have   b was   c had

5 Dogs are very _____ to their owners.
   a loyal   b friend   c stick

6 While she was taking a shower, somebody _____ her towel.
   a stole   b stolen   c was stealing

7 _____ my brother was born, we moved to a bigger house.
   a While   b When   c Then

8 My best friend and I fall _____ about twice a week, but we're soon friends again.
   a up   b out   c in

9 I _____ want to watch the movie because I had seen it three times before.
   a hadn't   b didn't   c wasn't

[ ] 8

3 Vocabulary

(Circle) the correct words.

1 A good friend will always stand *on* / (*by*) you, no matter what.

2 I think it's great the way you stick *up* / *out* for your friend.

3 He's not really a friend but more of an *acquaintance* / *old friend* – someone I work with.

4 I get *along* / *up* really well with all my teachers. I really like them.

5 Ali and I *hit* / *fell* it off as soon as we met. We've been friends ever since.

6 She's a really *close* / *open* friend. I tell her everything.

7 You don't need to thank me. That's *why* / *what* friends are for.

8 She feels you really *let* / *threw* her down. That's why's she's upset with you.

9 If you hit me again, I'm going to tell *on* / *out* you.

[ ] 8

How did you do?

Total: [ ] 25

 Very good
25 – 20

 OK
19 – 16

 Review Unit 4 again
15 or less

5 A working life

1 Grammar

✲ Present perfect vs. present perfect continuous review

a (Circle) the correct words.

1 Your brother has (written) / been writing three emails this morning.

2 I've *been taking / take* a technology course on the weekends. I have one more week to go.

3 I don't finish school for another year, but I've already *started / been starting* to look for a job.

4 Have you *seen / been seeing* the new James Bond movie?

5 My dad has always *had / been having* a thick beard.

6 What do you mean, you haven't had time to make dinner? What have you *done / been doing* all evening?

7 It's *snowed / been snowing* all night. Do you think it'll stop by tomorrow morning?

b Complete the sentences with the words in the box.

gone	been going	called	been calling
taken	been taking	painted	been painting

1 Her French is getting much better. She's *been going* to classes twice a week.

2 I've _____ three of the walls and both doors – just one more wall to go.

3 Kyle has _____ me seven times. I wonder what he wants.

4 He's _____ out, I'm afraid. If you want to wait, he'll be back in an hour.

5 I've _____ photos for the last two hours. The camera doesn't have any memory left now.

6 Have you _____ in here? It certainly smells like it.

7 Alisha's _____ you all day. Where have you been?

8 Who has _____ the last piece of cake? I wanted it!

c Match the dialogues and pictures, and then complete. Use the present perfect or present perfect continuous of the words in parentheses.

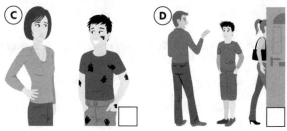

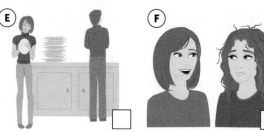

1 A: Where's your sister?

B: She _____'s gone_____ out with her friend. (go)

2 A: You look terrible! What's wrong?

B: Oh, I _____ (not sleep) well recently. Too much homework, I think!

3 A: Do you want another slice of this pizza? It's excellent.

B: No, thanks. I _____ enough. (eat)

4 A: I'm so sorry I'm late! How long _____ you _____ ? (wait)

B: Too long! I'm soaking wet.

5 A: What _____ you _____ ? (do)

B: Helping Dad change a tire on the car.

6 A: _____ you _____ (finish) doing the dishes yet?

B: No, not yet. _____ you _____ (see) how many dirty dishes there are?

d Complete the questions. Use the present perfect or present perfect continuous form of the verbs in the box.

do	have	~~go~~	download	save	know

1 So is that your new boyfriend? How long
   _____have you been going_____ out with him?

2 Nice phone, Jake. How long _____ it?

3 I didn't know you could water ski! How long
   _____ that?

4 I hear you want to buy a new sound system. How long
   _____ for it?

5 You didn't tell me you'd passed all of your exams!
   How long _____ ?

6 That video file is huge! How long _____
   it?

e Continue the biography of singer Katy Perry using the information below. Use the simple past and the present perfect or the present perfect continuous where appropriate.

- born in Santa Barbara, California (1984)
- name was Katheryn Hudson
- started singing at age nine
- moved to Nashville, Tennessee, to work with songwriters (1999)
- started learning to play the guitar for first album
- moved to Los Angeles, California, to work with a famous songwriter (2001)
- recorded her first album *Katy Hudson* (2001)
- started using the name Katy Perry (2004)
- recorded two more albums, *One of the Boys* and *Teenage Dream*

Katy Perry was born in 1984 in Santa Barbara, California. Her name was Katheryn Hudson. She has been singing since she was nine. She...

2 Grammar

✱ *had better / should / ought to*

a (Circle) the correct words in these sentences.

a You'd (better) / should / ought do it before Mom comes home!

b You *ought / better not / shouldn't* play with matches.

c You *ought / better not / shouldn't* let him use the Internet at night.

d You *better / should / ought* talk to some of your teachers about it.

e You'd *should / better / ought* wear some nice clothes. You need to look your best!

f You *ought / should / better* to look at the advertisements in the paper.

b Match the problems below with the advice in Exercise 2a. Write the letters a–g in the boxes.

1 "My son spends too much time
   in chat rooms." [c]

2 "I've burned my fingers." [ ]

3 "I want a good part-time job." [ ]

4 "I've got a job interview
   tomorrow." [ ]

5 "I don't know what career
   I want." [ ]

6 "I haven't cleaned my
   bedroom yet." [ ]

3 Pronunciation

✱ /ɔ/ *thought*

▶ **CD3 T22** Underline the words that have the /ɔ/ sound. Then listen and repeat.

1 I thought I saw you at the store.

2 We ought to go to the movies tonight.

3 Does your dad work in an office?

4 Did you chat online all night?

5 How long have you had that awful cold?

6 My brother played ball, and I went to the mall.

4 Vocabulary

⭑ Jobs and work

a Complete the crossword by solving the clues with words from page 33 of the Student's Book.

Across

4 Not working all of the working week
7 You have this if you've done the job before
9 Working the complete week
10 Leave a job
11 This is your money from work

Down

1 A worker for a company
2 Education, training and skills you have for a job
3 Without a job
5 Someone who is learning the skills of a job
6 Try to get a job
8 The person you work for

b Complete the two dialogues with words from the box.

> salary ~~qualifications~~ applied employer employees

Interviewer: Well, Ms. Lane, I see you graduated from Harvard, and you worked at L-Tech. Those are very impressive _qualifications_ . Why have you ¹_____ for a job with us?

Ms. Lane: I think you're a very fair ²_____ . You treat your ³_____ very well, from what I hear. And the ⁴_____ is excellent for a first job.

> ~~full-time~~ part-time resigned trainee unemployed

Interviewer: Are you working ___full-time___ at the moment, Alan?

Mr. Pitt: No, I'm not working at all. I've been ¹_____ for the last two weeks.

Interviewer: I see you ²_____ from your previous job in your first month as a ³_____ . What happened?

Mr. Pitt: The training program wasn't very good. I wanted to find something better.

Interviewer: I see. Well, we only have ⁴_____ jobs in your field at the moment – mornings, Monday to Friday, 20 hours a week. Would that interest you?

⭑ Fields of work

c Match the jobs 1–8 with the fields of work.

a public service _____5_____
b education _____
c entertainment _____
d health care _____
e technology and media _____
f legal _____
g finance _____
h management _____

Fiction in mind

a While you read the extract, choose the best word for each blank.

1	a computer	b (secretary)	c manager
2	a away	b about	c around
3	a Maybe	b However	c If
4	a work	b worked	c working
5	a told	b said	c spoke

You are going to read more of "The Book of Thoughts." Chester has discovered that the old book he found in the antique shop really does tell him what other people are thinking. But will this help him at work?

Chester walked into his office. His ¹ _secretary_ was already busy typing.

"Any messages, Miss Han?" he asked her.

"Yes, sir," said Miss Han, "from the manager. He says he can't go the meeting today about the Eastern business. He wants you to take over right ² _____."

Yes!

This was the kind of opportunity he'd been waiting for. He would show them all just how good he was. This was an important piece of business. ³ _____ he could make sure that everything went well, he would get noticed. He would be an obvious choice for the next manager's job. If he became a manager, he would be the youngest manager in the business! [...]

When he met the others, Chester was confident and did his job well. He made sure that everybody knew what to do. The meeting that afternoon was sure to be a success. If, of course, the figures he had were all correct.

Just then he noticed a little smile on the face of Mr. Shaw. "What's the old man got to smile about?" thought Chester. "He never smiles – why is he smiling now?" Then he remembered his little book.

He took it out of his pocket and hid it behind some papers. He pretended to be looking at his notes and thought of Mr. Shaw. The words appeared immediately:

I'll teach that young fool a lesson. I've got some figures he doesn't know about hidden in my office. I've been ⁴ _____ on this longer than he has. When he can't come up with the right figures, he'll look stupid. Then I'll produce them and save the day. He'll look like a boy trying to do a man's job. He needs to learn some respect for serious professionals like me.

Chester felt a cold sweat on the back of his neck.

"So the old man really does dislike me, after all!"

Chester wondered what all the others thought about him, but had no time to consult his book.

"Thanks, everybody – see you all this afternoon," Chester ⁵ _____ them all. "Enjoy your lunch."

(from Brennan, F. [2000] "The Book of Thoughts" in *The Fruitcake Special*, CUP: pp. 56–57)

b Choose the correct answer: a, b, c or d.

1 Why is Chester so pleased by his secretary's news?

  a He'll have the chance to take some time off.

  b He'll be able to work more closely with Mr. Shaw.

  c He'll have the chance to earn his manager's respect.

  d He'll be able to find out what his work colleagues think of him.

2 Why does Chester use the little book?

  a To check his figures for the meeting.

  b To read Mr. Shaw's thoughts.

  c To write what he thinks about the office employees.

  d To hide his figures from Mr. Shaw.

3 How does Chester feel at the end of the extract?

  a cold   b uncomfortable   c cheerful   d hungry

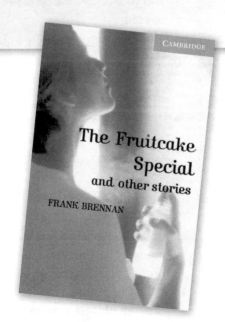

CAMBRIDGE

The Fruitcake Special
and other stories
FRANK BRENNAN

Skills in mind

6 Listen and write

a ▶ **CD3 T23** Listen to Chris describing a concert he saw, and complete the missing information.

b Match the underlined words and phrases a–d in the text with phrases 1–4.

1 all in all ☐

2 in conclusion ☐

3 was held ☐

4 well worth it ☐

WRITING TIP

Report writing

A report is similar to a description or review. It is normally written in a clear, semi-formal style, divided into paragraphs with headings to show what kind of information the reader will find. The report usually ends with a recommendation, which may contain your opinion.

- It helps to use headings for your paragraphs. You can then plan what you want to write, and your report will be easier to read.

- Try to learn useful words and expressions such as those underlined in the report and in Exercise 6b.

- Try to present your information as factually as you can, leaving your main opinions for the conclusion.

- In your conclusion, give a balanced assessment if possible. Be careful not to repeat what you wrote in previous paragraphs. If you are saying that you did not like something, try to find something positive to say.

Introduction

This report will describe a live event I attended recently. The event was a pop concert featuring ____10____ different singers and bands. Some of the money from ¹_____ sales was given to a charity for people with physical and mental disabilities.

Venue and cost

The concert ª took place at the Prudential Center in Newark, New Jersey. Tickets were ²_____, depending on where the seats were.

Atmosphere

At the beginning of the show, the sound wasn't ³_____. Later, the quality improved a lot. The lighting was very impressive. The crowd was very young. The average age was probably about ⁴_____.

Performances

Most of the performers played ⁵_____ songs. There were some delays between performances. The Black Eyed Peas were the main band. They played last. I thought Lady Gaga was the best performer. Her singing and dancing were excellent, and the audience responded very well.

Conclusion

ᵇ To sum it up, the show was ⁶_____ long, which was ᶜ good value for the money. Not all performers were equally good, though, and perhaps it would be a good idea to cut the number of performers. This show is touring the country, and my recommendation is that, if you like just two or three of the artists, you should definitely go and see it. ᵈ Overall, it was an excellent evening, with something for everyone.

c Your class is doing a survey on live events that they have attended (music concerts, dance and theater performances, craft fairs, sports, etc.). Write a report of 120–150 words about a live event you have seen, including:

- where the event was held
- the cost
- a general description
- what you liked/didn't like
- whether other people might like it
- a recommendation as to how it could be better

Unit check

1 Fill in the blanks

Complete the text with the words in the box.

| part-time | for | should | been | working | job | qualifications | experience | trainee | employee |

Everybody keeps asking me what kind of ....job............ I want to do when I finish school. My mom doesn't think I [1]...................... apply [2]...................... any jobs yet. She wants me to go to college and get the [3]...................... I need to be a teacher. My dad wants me to start [4]...................... for his bank as a(n) [5]....................... He says I could do the job [6]...................... to get some [7]......................, and go to college on my days off. I don't know if I want to be a(n) [8]...................... of a bank, though. I've [9]...................... thinking about maybe trying to sell some of my art. Decisions, decisions!

☐ 9

2 Choose the correct answers

(Circle) the correct answer: a, b or c.

1 How long have you been .... ?
   a resigning   b (unemployed)   c experienced

2 I really think you'd .... say sorry before it's too late.
   a should   b ought   c better

3 How long have you .... waiting for me?
   a just   b had   c been

4 Why don't you .... for that job? You might get it.
   a apply   b trainee   c employee

5 .... she be doing that?
   a Has   b Should   c Had

6 It looks like she .... been crying.
   a has   b just   c have

7 She's a good .... , and I like working for her.
   a employee   b women   c employer

8 I didn't get the job as I don't have enough work ....
   a trainee   b experience   c qualification

9 When do you think we .... to tell them we're leaving?
   a ought   b should   c better

☐ 8

3 Vocabulary

Match the two parts of the sentences. Write a–i in the boxes.

1 Volunteering is a good way   [g]   a apart from teaching.
2 If you don't like your job,   ☐   b out the application form.
3 You should apply   ☐   c to get into the legal field.
4 If you like, I'll help you fill   ☐   d you get a good job.
5 Good qualifications will help   ☐   e maybe you should resign.
6 There are other jobs in education   ☐   f for a public service job.
7 The entertainment field is more   ☐   g to get some experience.
8 I'd rather have my own business   ☐   h than just acting and singing.
9 Studying law is a good way   ☐   i than be somebody's employee.

☐ 8

How did you do?

Total: ☐ 25

| 😊 | Very good 25 – 20 | 😐 | OK 19 – 16 | 🙁 | Review Unit 5 again 15 or less |

6 Live forever!

1 Grammar
✱ Future predictions

a Complete the sentences with the correct form of *(not) be likely to*.

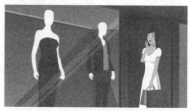

1 "It's nice, but it __'s likely__ __to__ be really expensive."

2 "Please write it down, because I _____ forget."

3 "You _____ fail the exam."

4 "He _____ play again for about six months."

5 "I _____ pass, am I?"

6 "Maybe we shouldn't play here. We _____ break something."

b Complete the sentences. Use the information in the chart.

100%	will	
75%	will probably	be likely to
50%	might	might not
25%	probably won't	not be likely to
0%	won't	

1 It / rain on the weekend. (75% + *will*)
   It will probably rain on the weekend.
2 My parents / be unhappy with my grades. (100%)
   ----
3 My brother / arrive late tomorrow. (75% + *likely*)
   ----
4 The game on Saturday / be very good. (0%)
   ----
5 I / go to the movies this evening. (50%)
   ----
6 I / pass next week's test. (75% + *likely*)
   ----
7 They / be at home tomorrow. (25% + *not likely*)
   ----

8 There / be much to eat at the party. (25% + *won't*)
   ----
9 We / visit our grandparents next weekend. (50% + *not*)
   ----

c Rewrite the sentences. Use the words in parentheses.

1 The chances of my father buying me a computer are small. (likely)
   My father isn't likely to buy me a computer.
2 It's possible that I will pass the exams. (might)
   ----
3 It's possible that he won't arrive on time. (might not)
   ----
4 I'm almost sure that I'll be late. (probably)
   ----
5 There isn't much of a chance my mother will lend me some money. (not likely)
   ----

6 I don't think that my sister will buy that car. (probably won't)

----

7 It's possible that he will be home. (likely)

----

2 Grammar

✱ First conditional review: *if* and *unless*

a Complete the sentences with the simple present form of the verbs or *will/won't*.

1 I _____will lend_____ (lend) you the money if you
_____promise_____ (promise) to give it back tomorrow.

2 If she _____ (call) me tonight,
I _____ (ask) her to go out with me.

3 The door _____ (not open) unless you
_____ (push) it hard.

4 Unless we _____ (leave) now, we
_____ (be) late for school.

5 If he _____ (not be) careful, he
_____ (hurt) himself.

6 I _____ (not come) if you
_____ (not want) me to.

7 Unless you _____ (stop) talking, the
teacher _____ (get) angry with you.

8 The dog _____ (not bite) you if you
_____ (leave) it alone.

b Make conditional sentences with the words.

1 you / have an accident / unless / you drive
more slowly
You'll have an accident unless you drive more
slowly.

2 If / John / invite me to the party, / I / go

----

3 I / beat Sally / unless / I / play badly

----

4 I / be very upset / if / he / lose my camera

----

5 Unless / you / go now, / the stores / be closed

----

6 If / my friend / come over, / we / play soccer

----

3 Grammar

✱ Time conjunctions: *if / unless / when / until / as soon as*

a (Circle) the correct words.

1 I'll tell you *until /* (*as soon as*) I know.

2 Mary isn't here yet so let's wait *until /
when* she arrives.

3 I'm going to buy a new computer *when /
unless* I have enough money.

4 You won't pass the test *if / unless* you
study more.

5 We'll go out *as soon as / unless* the
weather gets better.

6 I'll stay at home *as soon as / until* it stops
raining.

7 *When / Unless* we move to our new
house, I'll have my own bedroom.

8 *If / Until* I fail my driving test, I'll take it
again.

b Complete the sentences. Use *if, unless,
until* or *as soon as*.

1 She's coming home at 6:00. I'll talk to her
_____as soon as_____ she arrives.

2 _____ we hurry up, we'll be late
for the concert!

3 Dad's picking us up in the car, so we'll have
to wait _____ he gets here.

4 What will you do _____ you
don't pass your test?

5 Can you do me a favor? Take care of
my cat _____ I get back from
vacation, please.

6 I can't buy it _____ my parents
lend me some money.

7 I can't talk now, I'm watching a baseball
game, but I'll call you _____ it
finishes, OK?

8 _____ the movie theater is full,
don't worry. We can come back home and
watch a DVD.

Vocabulary

✱ Verbs with prepositions

a Find five words in the grid to complete the phrases.

G	A	R	G	E	T	T	I	N	G
R	R	E	O	V	T	H	N	E	R
O	G	A	R	R	H	I	R	A	E
W	O	R	R	Y	I	N	G	R	V
O	I	N	A	N	N	K	J	N	I
R	V	I	S	I	K	O	I	I	E
I	W	N	K	G	I	N	N	G	W
A	R	G	U	I	N	G	G	T	I
N	Y	R	R	I	G	O	I	R	N
C	E	T	J	T	I	N	G	S	G

Common causes of stress:

1 .... with people

2 .... about your problems

3 .... for the test

4 .... about what to wear

5 .... ready for school

b Look at the pictures. Complete the sentences with the expressions from Exercise 4a.

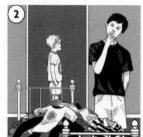

4 Don't sit there .... Go and do something about them!

5 He's a really unpleasant guy. He's always .... and fighting.

c Complete the sentences with the correct prepositions.

1 I'm pretty worried ___*about*___ my sister.

2 My parents are thinking .... moving to another town.

3 School ends next week, so I'm getting ready .... summer vacation.

4 Are you reviewing .... our test right now?

5 Why are you always arguing .... your parents?

6 What are you waiting .... ?

1 I hate ___*getting ready*___ for school! I almost always forget a book or something.

2 My brother's going to a party tonight, and he's spent hours ....

3 I think .... is pointless! Either you've learned the things already, or you haven't!

5 Pronunciation

✱ Prepositions

▶ **CD3 T24** Listen and repeat. Pay particular attention to the underlined words.

1 I'm looking <u>for</u> my books.

2 What are you waiting <u>for</u>?

3 Sorry. I don't want to talk <u>to</u> you.

4 Who are you writing <u>to</u>?

5 Are you looking <u>at</u> me?

6 Who are you looking <u>at</u>?

6 | **Vocabulary bank** Complete the cartoons with the correct prepositions.

1 "I'd like to apply ___for___ the job of bank manager."

2 "My son doesn't like some of the parents I hang out _____."

3 "I don't think I'll go _____ dessert, thanks."

4 "We can only hope _____ someone to find us soon."

5 "Do you think they'll have anything to talk _____?"

6 "We'll probably be able to laugh _____ it one day."

---

7 ## Study help

✱ Learning and recording words in context

- It's very important to record words that you learn in a context. In other words, don't record them as words on their own.

- For example: if you learn the verb "worry," you <u>could</u> record it as one word and then write a translation, e.g., "worry = preoccupied."

- But in order to <u>use</u> the word "worry," you need to know and remember words that go with it – e.g., the preposition "about." So it's

much better to write a sentence or phrase that uses the other words, too, e.g., "She never seems to worry about anything." (You can add a translation if you think it's important and useful.)

- It's also a good idea to record <u>your own</u> sentences/phrases about things that are true for you. This makes new language much easier to remember.

Write sentences/phrases in your notebook (or here) that will help you remember and use these words from the unit:

argue ....

get ready ....

unless ....

as soon as ....

likely ....

Skills in mind

8 Write

a Read this advertisement in a newspaper. The advertisement requests information about four different things. What are they?

b A young man named Mario wrote a letter to apply for one of the jobs. Read his letter and say which of the four requests for information in the advertisement he <u>doesn't</u> respond to.

Dear Sir or Madam,

I am writing to apply for a summer camp job in the United States.

I am an independent and reliable person. [1]<u>Unless I get one of the jobs</u>, I will work hard, and I am sure that I will be a good employee.

I think that you need patience and a good sense of humor to work with younger children. I believe I have these qualities, but I also think that [2]<u>they are likely improve</u> through this work. I think I will also learn how to deal with difficult children, and to provide discipline when it is needed.

It has always been my dream to visit the United States. I believe that my English will improve, and I am sure that I [3]<u>will to learn</u> a lot of things about a different and foreign culture.

[4]<u>Thank you for consider</u> my application. I look forward to your reply.

Sincerely,

Mario Gomez

c Each of the <u>underlined</u> phrases 1–4 contains a language mistake. Correct each one.

d Imagine that you want to apply for one of the summer camp jobs. Write your letter in about 120–180 words. (Don't count the opening and your name.)

SUMMER CAMPS in the U.S.

Wanted: young people to work at a vacation camp for 10- to 13-year-old children in the United States for three months. Various locations in the country. The work includes organizing entertainment for the children and general cleaning duties.

If you are interested in this position, write and tell us:

- why you think you are suitable for the job
- about your level of English
- what you think you will gain from working with younger children
- what you think you will gain or learn from being in the U.S. for three months

Write to PO Box 788, Bar Harbor, Maine, 04609, before April 30 this year.

WRITING TIP

Writing a letter for an exam

When you write a letter, especially for a test or an examination, remember that you should always:

- Read the task carefully and do exactly what it asks you to do. In this example, you need to read the advertisement carefully and make sure that you provide all the information that the advertisement asks for. If you leave out important information, you will lose a lot of points.

- Check your own writing carefully when you have finished. Check for grammar mistakes and for any spelling mistakes. During tests especially, it is easy to make small mistakes under pressure. Give yourself time at the end to check.

- Check your text, if there is a word limit, to make sure that you have used about the required number of words. If you don't write enough words, you will lose points. If you write too many, the person grading the test might not read the whole thing.

Unit check

1 Fill in the blanks

Complete the text with the words in the box.

| until   if   unless   likely   might   probably   for   about   ~~when~~   with |

I'm not very sure what to do _____*when*_____ I finish school. ¹_____ I do well on my exams,
I ²_____ go to college, but I ³_____ won't get good enough grades. I haven't been studying enough
this year. For example, I never study ⁴_____ a test before I take it. So I think that maybe I'll get a job, save
some money and then travel ⁵_____ I don't have any money left. When I told my parents about that,
they weren't very happy, and they argued ⁶_____ me for a long time. They said they were worried
⁷_____ me, and they didn't want me to go. And I don't think they're ⁸_____ to change their minds.
So, ⁹_____ I can think of something else, I still won't know what to do when I finish school! | 9 |

2 Choose the correct answers

Circle the correct answer: a, b or c.

1 _____ the weather's nice this weekend,
   we can have a picnic.
   a (If) b When c As soon as

2 Why do you always argue _____ me?
   a to b at c with

3 I can't go out tonight. I'm studying _____
   a test.
   a for b about c to

4 I don't want to leave. I want to stay _____
   the movie finishes.
   a until b if c when

5 I'll call you as soon as I _____ anything.
   a am hearing b will hear c hear

6 I can't stand her because she only ever thinks _____
   herself.
   a for b about c with

7 They won't know _____ you don't tell them.
   a unless b when c if

8 Mike's upstairs _____ ready for tonight's party.
   a going b getting c being

9 You won't pass the test _____ you study hard.
   a as soon as b when c unless | 8 |

3 Vocabulary

Circle the correct words.

1 What a cool camera! We're going to have
   some fun (with) / for it.

2 I had a great chat by / with my dad last
   night. He's not as old as I thought!

3 If / When you had a lot of money, what
   would you do?

4 Let's search for / with the answer on the
   Internet.

5 I dreamed about / by you last night. It was
   a really weird dream.

6 I can't go out tonight. I have to review about /
   for a test.

7 We're in a hurry. We have to leave until / as soon as
   we've had lunch.

8 It took her hours to get ready for / by the party.
   Was it worth it?

9 I won't help you unless / if you say sorry for
   being mean to me this morning. | 8 |

How did you do?

Total: | 25 |

| | Very good 25 – 20 | | OK 19 – 16 | 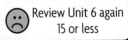 | Review Unit 6 again 15 or less |

1 Grammar

✱ make / let / be allowed to

a Put the words in the correct order to make sentences.

1 a noise / aren't / to / You / make / allowed
   You aren't allowed to make a noise.

2 travelers / to / The / allowed / enter / weren't / the country
   ....

3 parents / play outside / let / Our / never / us
   ....

4 us / The / didn't / leave / early / let / teacher
   ....

5 cell / made / turn off / our / They / us / phones
   ....

6 make / Do / before / your parents / bed / you / to / go / 10 o'clock?
   ....

b Look at the signs. Write sentences with *(not) allowed to.*

1 *You aren't allowed to*
  ride your bike here.

2 ....
  ....

3 ....
  ....

4 ....
  ....

5 ....
  ....

6 ....
  but ....

c Rewrite the sentences. Use the words in parentheses.

1 We don't have permission to go into that room. (allow)
   We *aren't allowed to go into*
   that room.

2 The teacher told us to stay longer at school yesterday. (make)
   The teacher ....
   ....

3 I don't allow my sister to borrow my things. (let)
   I ....
   ....

4 My father didn't give me permission to borrow his car. (let)
   My father ....
   ....

5 You can't park your car here. (allow)
   You ....
   ....

6 My mom says I have to pay for my own cell phone. (make)
   My mom ....
   ....

2 Vocabulary

✱ Television

a Match the words with the definitions. Write 1–8 in the boxes.

> 1 episode 2 ~~series~~ 3 celebrities 4 ratings 5 audience
> 6 sitcoms 7 host 8 viewer 9 contestant 10 quiz show

a a group of shows about the same
subject [2]

b comedy shows about the lives of ordinary
people [ ]

c a person who takes part in a quiz show [ ]

d one show in a series [ ]

e the person who presents a show [ ]

f people who watch a TV show
in the studio [ ]

g the number of people who watch
a TV show [ ]

h a show where people answer
questions [ ]

i a person who is watching a TV
show at home (not in the studio) [ ]

j well-known people on television
(or in movies) [ ]

b Complete the sentences with the correct form of the words at the end of each line.

Yesterday evening, I watched a ___wonderful___ new quiz show on TV. There are   WONDER

four [1] _____ who have to answer really hard questions that the host   CONTEST

asks them. If they don't know the answer to a question, they are [2] _____   ALLOW

to call home and get some help. And sometimes the [3] _____ at home   VIEW

can call the show and ask questions, too. The [4] _____ gets   WIN

a new car as a prize! I think it's going to be a very [5] _____ show.   SUCCESS

The [6] _____ are already high.   RATE

3 Pronunciation

✱ /aʊ/ all<u>ow</u>ed

a ▶ CD3 T25 Check (✔) the words
that have the sound /aʊ/ in them.
Then listen, check and repeat.

1 how	✔	6 shout	[ ]
2 know	[ ]	7 slow	[ ]
3 now	[ ]	8 house	[ ]
4 mouse	[ ]	9 found	[ ]
5 loud	[ ]	10 snow	[ ]

b ▶ CD3 T26 Listen and repeat.

1 How do you know which house it is?

2 I found a mouse in the snow.

3 We heard a loud shout.

4 There was a mouse running loudly
around the house.

4 Grammar

✱ Modal verbs of obligation, prohibition
and permission

a Complete the sentences with the words in the box.

> have to go   must not go   can't bring
> don't have to stay   can stay   ~~must bring~~

1 "Tomorrow afternoon is music, so you
___must bring___ your instruments, OK?"

2 "Great! My dad says I _____ out as late
as I want to."

3 "Sorry, I'm really late for my meeting.
I _____ now."

4 "Are you bored? Well, look, you _____
here if you don't want to."

5 "Hey, Alex, that's the girls' bathroom. You
_____ in there!"

6 "Sorry, you _____ your dog into the
library. No animals are allowed in here."

Look at the pictures. What are the people saying? Complete the sentences.

1 "We __can't__ leave through here."

2 "You _____ feed the animals!"

3 "You _____ open it now if you want."

4 "We _____ show something to prove we're 18."

5 "I _____ clean up this mess!"

6 "Great! I _____ wear a suit and tie!"

5 Vocabulary

✱ Extreme adjectives and modifiers

a Complete the sentences with the words in the box.

fantastic	enormous	awful	boiling	exhausted
hilarious	~~tiny~~	starving	freezing	fascinating

1 A: My dog is so small and cute!
   B: Small? She's ____tiny____!

2 A: Was it really hot in Australia?
   B: Yes, it was! In fact, it was _____.

3 A: This is a good song.
   B: Yes, it's _____.

4 A: Is it cold outside?
   B: It's _____.

5 A: Is her new apartment very big?
   B: It certainly is. In fact, it's _____.

6 A: Are you still feeling bad?
   B: Yes, I feel really _____.

7 A: He's so funny!
   B: I know. He's _____.

8 A: What an interesting story!
   B: Yes, it was _____.

9 A: Are you hungry?
   B: I'm _____!

10 A: I think they're tired.
   B: Tired? They're _____!

---

b **Vocabulary bank** Respond to the questions with *Yes*, an adjective from the box and *absolutely, very* or *really*. More than one answer is possible.

~~disgusting~~	delicious	deafening
terrible	terrified	thrilled

1 The pizza was bad, wasn't it?
   Yes, it was absolutely disgusting.

2 Were you scared by that thunder?
   _____

3 Was the band really loud?
   _____

4 Is the soup tasty?
   _____

5 Are you excited about Disneyland?
   _____

6 Is it really bad news?
   _____

6 Vocabulary

✱ Making new friends

Replace the underlined words with phrasal verbs from the box.

feel left out	bond with	fit in
join in		

1 Karen's playing with her new puppy. She's trying to <u>make a close connection with</u> it.

   _____

2 What's wrong with you, Sam? Don't you want to <u>be part of</u> the game?

   _____

3 I'm not going out with James and his friends any more. I just don't <u>feel like I belong</u>.

   _____

4 Here's a present for you, Tomas. I don't want you to <u>think you're not being included</u>.

   _____

7 Culture in mind

a Read the text about a song. Some of the lines of the text have an extra, unnecessary word. Write the word at the end of the line. If the line is correct, check (✔) it.

"Somebody's Watching Me" by Rockwell

The song "Somebody's Watching Me" <u>it</u> was recorded by a singer named	1	*it*
Rockwell. Rockwell was in fact a man named Kennedy Gordy, who was	2	✔
the son of Berry Gordy, the man who he started Motown Records.	3	
Gordy changed his the name because he wanted to make records, but he	4	
also did wanted to be recognized for his talent. He signed with Motown	5	
as a solo artist without his father's knowledge, and took his name from his	6	
high school band. Rockwell's sister, Hazel, was married to the Jermaine Jackson,	7	
Michael Jackson's brother, and that's why Rockwell was able to can get Michael	8	
and Jermaine to sing with on the recording. The song was a big hit and went	9	
to number 2 on the charts in 1984. Rockwell then revealed his true identity.	10	
But he didn't have much more success, and his next album didn't sell well not at all.	11	

b Read the text again. Mark the statements *T* (true), *F* (false) or *N* (information not given).

1 Rockwell's real name was Berry Gordy. — F

2 Motown Records started in Detroit, in the United States. ☐

3 Berry Gordy knew that his son had signed with Motown. ☐

4 Jermaine Jackson was Rockwell's brother-in-law. ☐

5 "Somebody's Watching Me" was a successful single. ☐

6 Rockwell's next album sold less than ten thousand copies. ☐

c ▶ CD3 T27 Listen to Dave telling a friend about the video for "Somebody's Watching Me". Put the pictures in the correct order. Write numbers 1–6 in the boxes.

7

d Here are three lines from the song. Which pictures are they related to?

1 But maybe showers remind me of *Psycho* too much.

2 Well, can the people on TV see me or am I just paranoid?

3 Well, is the mailman watching me?

8 Write

a Josh and Sarah had to write articles for their school magazine. Do not write anything yet, but read what they had to do:

> **Write an article about your favorite television show. Write about:**
>
> • the kind of show it is, and how often it is on TV
> • who the people in the show are
> • what the show is about
> • what you especially like in the show and why
> • who you would recommend it to
>
> **Write between 120 and 150 words.**

b Read Josh's and Sarah's articles. Complete the sentences with the words from the box.

> get to know   know each other
> especially   no matter
> ~~moved in~~

c Which of the two articles do you think is better? Why?

d Write an article for your school magazine. Use the same task as Josh and Sarah's.

My favorite show is *Two and a Half Men*. It's a show about two men who are brothers. Charlie lived alone for a long time, but then his brother Alan ___*moved in*___ with his son Jake. Charlie is relaxed and outgoing while Alan is uptight and nervous all the time. They don't always get along, but they both love Jake and want what's best for him.

I love the show because the guys are really funny, [1]_____ Jon Cryer, the actor who plays Alan. There is always a problem, but they usually work it out.

The show is on once a week, and I watch it on Mondays at 9:00 p.m. (Josh – 111 words)

My favorite show is a reality TV show called *Big Brother*. It's on three times a week, on Wednesday, Thursday and Sunday evenings. In the show, 13 people have to live in a house together, and they don't [2]_____ before the show. Each week, they decide who has to leave the house, and the last person to leave wins $500,000. The show

started in 2000, so it's been on TV for more than 10 years now!

I like *Big Brother* because the people are really fascinating, and you [3]_____ about their lives. They have complex problems like real people, and they don't always get along. I think that anyone who enjoys knowing about other people would love *Big Brother*. There's something for everyone — [4]_____ who you are! You'll have your favorite houseguest, and it's fun to see who makes it to the end.   (Sarah – 146 words)

WRITING TIP

Organizing a writing task

When you are given a writing task, make sure you follow the order of things you are asked to do. This will help you organize your writing.

Look at Josh's article, for example. Here is what he talks about, in this order:

a the name of the show
b what it's about
c what the characters are like
d why he likes the show
e what the characters are like (again)
f when the show is on

Does Josh write about all the topics he is asked to write about?

Compare Josh's answer to Sarah's. Check:

a what the task asks for
b the information Sarah includes in her answer and the order in which she presents it

1 Fill in the blanks

Complete the text with the words in the box.

> allowed   awful   ~~contestants~~   episodes   hilarious   host   huge   makes   winner   viewers

I like to watch videos of a Japanese game show called *Endurance*. On the show, the _contestants_ have different contests. There is a ¹_____ , and he ²_____ them do unpleasant things for the contests. Some of the things are really ³_____ ! I remember in one of the ⁴_____ , people had to ride bikes with hot spice in their mouths. They weren't ⁵_____ to drink any water. The person who rode the longest was the ⁶_____ . The show was on TV in the 1980s, and many people thought it was ⁷_____ . I think it's pretty funny, too. It didn't have a lot of ⁸_____ in the '80s, but now a ⁹_____ amount of people watch it on the Internet.

| 9 |

2 Choose the correct answers

Circle the correct answer: a, b or c.

1 The _____ in the studio enjoyed the show a lot.
   a viewing   b (audience)   c ratings

2 We don't like wearing a uniform, but the school _____ us wear one.
   a makes   b lets   c allowed

3 This soap opera has the highest _____ of any TV show in history!
   a viewers   b ratings   c contestants

4 The water was so cold. In fact, it was _____ !
   a starving   b boiling   c freezing

5 It's a vacation day today, so we _____ go to school.
   a don't have to   b must   c have to

6 I watched the first six _____ of the series, but then I got bored.
   a ratings   b celebrities   c episodes

7 One day I want to be a _____ on a quiz show. I'm sure I'd win!
   a host   b viewer   c contestant

8 A few minutes ago, I was hungry, but now I'm absolutely _____ !
   a tiny   b starving   c exhausted

9 My school doesn't _____ us to stay inside at break time.
   a let   b make   c allow

| 8 |

3 Vocabulary

Replace the underlined words so that the sentences make sense.

1 That movie was absolutely <u>boring</u>. I laughed all the way through it. _____hilarious_____

2 Come over and <u>bond</u> in the fun. _____

3 The forest fire was enormous. I was really <u>delicious</u>. _____

4 I'm really <u>excited</u>. I could go to sleep right now. _____

5 Your handwriting is so <u>deafening</u> I can't read it. _____

6 I don't <u>feel comfortable</u> here. I'm so different from everyone else. _____

7 That's a(n) <u>absolutely</u> good idea. _____

8 He was the <u>audience</u> on that wildlife show, but I can't remember his name. _____

9 She's an absolutely <u>disgusting</u> singer. I think she's my favorite. _____

| 8 |

How did you do?

Total: | 25 |

| 😊 | Very good 25 – 20 | 😐 | OK 19 – 16 | 🙁 | Review Unit 7 again 15 or less |

8 Survival

1 Grammar

✱ Present passive and past passive review

a (Circle) the correct answer: a, b, c or d.

1 Hockey is a popular sport that _____ indoors.
   a plays   b (is played)   c played   d was played

2 President John Kennedy _____ in Dallas in November 1963.
   a kills   b is killed   c killed   d was killed

3 Many Japanese people _____ sushi and sashimi.
   a eat   b are eaten   c ate   d were eaten

4 Many animals _____ for scientific experiments in the past.
   a use   b are used   c used   d were used

5 Spanish _____ by a lot of people in the U.S.
   a speaks   b is spoken   c spoke   d was spoken

6 Honda is a company that _____ cars.
   a makes   b is made   c made   d was made

b Write sentences using the present passive or past passive.

1 The World Trade Center / destroy / on September 11, 2001
   The World Trade Center was destroyed on September 11, 2001.

2 A language called Hindi / speak / in many parts of India _____

3 The 2008 Olympic Games / hold / in Beijing _____

4 Boeing 747 planes / call / jumbos _____

5 Most American movies / make / in Hollywood _____

6 The 2006 soccer World Cup / win / by Italy _____

7 John Lennon / kill / in December 1980 _____

8 The *Titanic* / sink / by an iceberg _____

9 Gorillas / find / in the forests of Africa _____

10 Buildings / design / by architects _____

2 Grammar

✱ Causative *have* (*have something done*)

a Look at the signs. Write sentences about what you can have done at each place.

1 You can *have your pizza delivered.*

2 You can have your _____
   _____ .

3 You can _____
   _____ .

4 You _____
   _____ .

5 You _____
   _____ .

6 _____
   _____ .

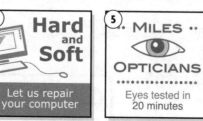

b ▶ CD3 T28 Look at the pictures and write the sentences. Choose words from the box. Then listen and check.

> photograph ~~test~~ computer repair car take ~~eyes~~ build garage deliver

1 She *'s having her eyes tested.* 2 They _____. 3 He _____.

4 She _____. 5 They _____.

Pronunciation

❋ Stress pattern in *have something done*

a ▶ CD3 T28 Listen again to the sentences in Exercise 2b. Mark the stressed words.

b ▶ CD3 T28 Listen again and repeat the sentences.

4 # Vocabulary

❋ *make* and *do*

a Match the two parts of the sentences. Write a–h in the boxes.

1 Eat fruit! It'll do | [d] | a sense to me!
2 I dropped some paint on the floor, and it made | [ ] | b fun of other people.
3 It's not nice to make | [ ] | c a real mess.
4 You can do it if you make | [ ] | d you some good.
5 She was very funny, but I did | [ ] | e a lot of money.
6 I don't want to invite Greg. He always makes | [ ] | f my best not to laugh at her.
7 When he sold his house, he made | [ ] | g trouble at parties.
8 Why is she always late? It doesn't make | [ ] | h an effort.

b Complete the sentences with the correct form of *make* or *do*.

1 Don't just sit there! __Do__ something!

2 I took the medicine the doctor gave me, and it _____ me a lot of good.

3 I've read this page three times, and it still _____ (not) sense to me!

4 I have a faster computer now, and it _____ a big difference.

5 Yesterday's test was hard! But I _____ my best.

6 There was a group of boys trying to _____ trouble at the game.

7 I think I _____ a mess of the interview. I didn't know what to say.

8 I'm going to get a job and _____ some money.

c **Vocabulary bank** (Circle) the correct words.

1 That didn't go very well. Let's go home and make a fresh (start) / room tomorrow.

2 I'm interested in the bike you have for sale. I'd like to make you *a price / an offer*.

3 If you want a sofa in your room, you're going to have to take something out to make *spare / room* for it.

4 Mom, we want to make a *question / request*: Can we go on a picnic this weekend, please?

5 Paul, your father and I need to talk to you. Can you make some *room / time* to sit down with us later today?

6 Sabrina just got a job as a fashion designer. What a great way to make a *living / job*!

7 Please go back and make *definite / sure* that you locked the front door.

8 The city is planning to knock down some houses to make *way / route* for a new highway.

5 Grammar

✶ Present perfect passive

a Complete the sentences with the words in the box.

> have been hurt   has been made
> have been sold   have been made
> haven't been invited   ~~has been built~~

1 A new library ___has been built___ in our town.

2 Their new CD only came out last week, but thousands of copies _____ already!

3 There's been an earthquake in our country, and a lot of people _____ .

4 Many animals _____ extinct in the last twenty years.

5 They're having a party tomorrow evening, but we _____ !

6 A big effort _____ recently to keep the town clean.

b What has happened in each picture? Complete the sentences with the present perfect passive form of the verbs in parentheses.

1 The woman ___has been robbed___ . (rob)

2 Three houses _____ . (knock down)

3 Their pizzas _____ (not deliver) yet.

4 The bank robbers _____ . (catch)

5 That car _____ (not clean) for weeks!

6 The fire _____ . (put out)

c Rewrite the sentences to make them passive.

1 A man from Boston has won the $25 million jackpot.
The $25 million jackpot *was won by a man in Boston.*

2 Messi scored the winning goal.
The winning goal _____ .

3 A professional decorated our house.
Our house _____ .

4 They didn't deliver our passports to us in time.
Our passports _____ .

5 Mr. Brown deals with all complaints.
All complaints _____ .

6 Mary always cut my hair.
I _____ .

6 Grammar

✱ Future passive

a Look at the poster. What will be done if they are elected? Complete the sentences.

1 New schools ___will be built___ .

2 Trees and parks _____ .

3 Taxes _____ .

4 Food _____ to poor families.

5 More police officers _____ on the streets.

6 Hospitals _____ .

7 New companies _____ .

8 Pollution _____ .

VOTE FOR US!

We will …
- build new schools!
- protect trees and parks!
- NOT increase taxes!
- give food to poor families!
- put more police officers on the streets!
- NOT close hospitals!
- help new companies!
- reduce pollution!

b Complete the sentences/questions. Use the future passive form of the verbs in parentheses.

1 A new swimming pool ___will be built___ (build) in our town next year.

2 It _____ (not finish) until next October.

3 _____ the water _____ (heat)?

4 All the swimmers _____ (supervise) by lifeguards.

5 Children under 10 _____ (not allow) to swim without an adult.

6 _____ people who can't swim _____ (give) lessons?

7 Everyday English

a Complete the expressions with the words in the box.

~~mean~~ Any How More all earth

1 I ___mean___

2 What on _____ (are you doing)?

3 _____ chance (you could help me)?

4 after _____

5 _____ come (you're late)?

6 _____ or less

b Complete the dialogues with the expressions in Exercise 7a.

1 A: I got the last question wrong.
   B: But it was so easy! _____ you didn't know the answer?

2 A: Like my new coat? It cost me $200!
   B: $200?? That's really expensive! _____ are you doing, buying things like that?

3 A: Have you finished that book?
   B: _____ . I just have the last 10 pages to read.

4 A: Hi, David. What's the matter?
   B: Hi, Mr. Jones. The thing is, I missed my bus. _____ you could take me to school?

5 A: He won't lend me his MP3 player! I don't understand why not.
   B: Well, maybe he's using it. And it's his MP3 player, _____ .

6 A: You made a complete mess of everything!
   B: Oh, come on. That's not fair. _____ , I did my best.

8 Listen

▶ **CD3 T29** Listen to five short recordings. For each one, (circle) the correct answer: a, b or c.

1 Listen to a teacher who is talking to a group of students about a bus. What time will the bus leave?

  a 8:15

  b 8:30

  c 8:50

2 Listen to a teacher talking to a girl, Sally, about her test grades. What does the math teacher think about Sally's grades?

  a She's very happy with Sally's progress.

  b She thinks that Sally could make more progress.

  c She's very angry that Sally hasn't made progress.

3 Mike is talking to Andrea. What is different about Andrea?

  a She's had her hair cut.

  b She's had her arm tattooed.

  c She's had her ears pierced.

4 A news announcer is talking about an earthquake. How many people have been killed?

  a About four thousand.

  b About four hundred.

  c About fourteen thousand.

5 Listen to a phone conversation. A woman is ordering a pizza. How much will she have to pay for the pizza?

  a $14.50 plus 50¢ for delivery.

  b $14.50 if she wants the pizza in the next 30 minutes.

  c Nothing if the pizza is not delivered within 30 minutes.

LISTENING TIP

How to answer multiple-choice questions

- Read all the choices carefully and make sure you understand them. What do you have to listen for? For example, in number 1 you have to listen for a time.

- Remember that you will need to listen to the whole section before you choose your answer. Never write down the first thing you hear. For example, in number 1, the man tells the students to be back at the bus at 8:15, but that isn't when the bus will leave. He then goes on to say it will leave "at eight thirty." So, what time does the bus leave?

- Remember that you can usually hear the recording twice. Use the second listening either to check your answer, or to help you think about the correct answer.

1 Fill in the blanks

Complete the text with the words in the box.

were	was	have	had	~~went~~	developed
made	made	taken	effort		

Last year I needed a new passport, so I ___went___ to a store in town and had my photograph
[1]_____ . When I went back two days later to get the photo, I looked at it and thought it
[2]_____ awful! The color was strange, and I was sure it hadn't been [3]_____ properly, so I
complained to the man in the store. I said: "You've [4]_____ a mess of this!" Then he [5]_____ fun
of me! The manager asked me if I wanted to [6]_____ my photo taken again. I wasn't very happy, but
I said OK, sat down and made a big [7]_____ to smile. This time I [8]_____ three photos taken,
but when I saw them they [9]_____ worse than the first one because I looked so angry!   [9]

2 Choose the correct answers

Circle the correct answer: a, b or c.

1 Work hard and you'll _____ money.
   a do   b (make)   c have

2 I need to throw some old clothes away to make
   _____ for the new ones.
   a room   b a mess   c an effort

3 My dad's car broke down, so he had to _____
   it repaired.
   a have   b do   c make

4 If you pronounce a language well, it makes a big
   _____ for other people.
   a mess   b difference   c progress

5 A prehistoric man _____ last year.
   a was found   b find   c is found

6 She went to the salon to _____ .
   a cut her hair   b have cut her hair
   c have her hair cut

7 Eating fruit can do you a lot of _____ .
   a best   b good   c better

8 Since last year, a lot of new roads _____ .
   a have been built   b were built   c have built

9 The government says that next year,
   taxes will _____ .
   a reduce   b be reduced   c have reduced

   [8]

3 Vocabulary

Complete the dialogue. Write one word in each space.

Pam: Hey, Lucy. Have you heard that they want
to knock down the swimming pool to make
___way___ for a new mall?

Lucy: No way! Well, I think we should all make
a big [1]_____ to stop them! I'm fed up
with the planners making a [2]_____ of
our town.

Pam: I agree! I'll do my [3]_____ to get
some of our friends involved. Like Gerry.

Lucy: There's no point in asking Gerry. He'll just
make [4]_____ of what we're trying to
do. He always laughs at us anyway.

Pam: I don't care. We're going to try to
[5]_____ some good in this town. If he
wants to [6]_____ trouble, or tease us
about it, that's up to him.

Lucy: OK, well, first of all, let's talk to our parents
and see what ideas they have.

Pam: Yes, that makes [7]_____ . They always
have good ideas. Let's talk to them now. I want
to make [8]_____ we do something
about this!   [8]

How did you do?

Total: [25]

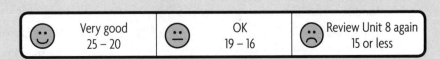

| ☺ Very good 25 – 20 | ☹ OK 19 – 16 | ☹ Review Unit 8 again 15 or less |

1 Grammar

✱ Gerunds and infinitives

a Find and (circle) seven verbs that are followed by a gerund (→ ←) and seven verbs that are followed by the infinitive. (↓ ↑)

W	T	R	E	N	J	O	Y	E	E
P	N	O	U	X	G	F	L	P	S
R	A	W	F	I	O	F	O	V	O
O	W	M	I	S	S	E	D	E	O
M	I	N	D	E	E	R	R	J	H
I	M	A	G	I	N	E	O	L	C
S	U	G	G	E	S	T	F	E	H
E	K	I	L	L	E	E	F	A	O
P	S	E	C	I	T	C	A	R	P
O	A	E	V	I	L	O	S	N	E

b Complete the sentences with the gerund or infinitive form of the verbs in parentheses. Then look at page 58 of the Student's Book to check your answers.

1 In *To Kill a Mockingbird*, Atticus Finch decides ____*to defend*____ (defend) an African American man named Tom Robinson.

2 Atticus shows that Mayella has avoided _____ (tell) the truth about Tom.

3 In *Frankenstein*, Victor Frankenstein tries _____ (create) a perfect human.

4 Instead, Victor creates an ugly monster that people can't stand _____ (look) at.

5 Victor's monster tries _____ (make) friends, but he can't.

6 The monster feels like _____ (kill) Victor.

7 The monster doesn't manage _____ (kill) Victor, but he kills Victor's wife and brother.

8 Then Victor promises _____ (dedicate) his life to saving the world from the monster.

c Complete the text with the correct form of the verbs in the box.

> write be read ~~learn~~ help fight
> kill play

Everyone knows about Sherlock Holmes, the famous British detective, who enjoyed ____*learning*____ about the law and who practiced [1] _____ his violin while he thought about his latest case. Not so many people are familiar with his enemy, Professor Moriarty.

Whereas Holmes promised [2] _____ evil, Moriarty chose [3] _____ evil. In fact, Moriarty offered [4] _____ all the criminals in London.

When Holmes' creator, Sir Arthur Conan Doyle, didn't feel like [5] _____ any more detective stories, he decided [6] _____ both characters. In a famous scene from *The Final Problem* (1893), Moriarty and Holmes fell to their deaths while fighting on top of the Reichenbach waterfalls in Switzerland.

However, under pressure from his readers who missed [7] _____ about their favorite detective, Conan Doyle brought Holmes back to life for the 1903's book *The Adventure of the Empty House*. So did Moriarty really die? Only one man knows.

d Put the words in the correct order to make sentences.

1 friends / I / really / with / enjoy / time / spending / my

I really enjoy spending time with my friends.

2 again / see / I / to / you / want / soon

....

3 help / school / to / My / offered / me / after / teacher

....

4 called / being / can't stand / Timothy / He

....

5 imagine / with / I / getting / angry / can't / him

....

6 to / more / to / have / patient / learn / You'll / be

....

e Complete the sentences with verbs from Box A and Box B in the correct forms.

Box A	Box B
feel like miss practice afford avoid mind ~~offer~~ promise	give go speak buy live get up study ~~lend~~

1 Dad ____offered____ ____to lend____ me his car for the weekend. Where should we go?

2 I really don't .... to school today. I want to stay in bed all day!

3 I can't .... a new computer. I've only saved $300.

4 This city's so noisy. I really .... by the ocean.

5 She .... me her answer tomorrow. I hope she says "yes."

6 I need someone .... French with. I have my oral test next week.

7 I don't .... early, but I prefer to sleep in on the weekends.

8 I always .... the night before a test.

2 Vocabulary

✱ Noun suffixes

a Write the noun forms of the words in the box in the correct columns.

kind   popular   ~~relax~~   protect   prefer   probable   react
enjoy   prepare   imagine   agree   differ   entertain   possible

-ation	-ence	-ment	-ness	-ion	-ity
relaxation					

b Complete the text with the correct form of the words.

James Bond's ___popularity___ is as big as it has ever been. Today's audiences continue to [1] .... 007, a half a century after his first appearance in 1962's _Dr No_.

Bond still offers the world [2] .... from villains by using his [3] ....

Young or old, male or female, audiences all [4] .... that Bond movies are still great [5] ....

POPULAR
ENJOYMENT

PROTECT
IMAGINE
AGREEMENT
ENTERTAIN

c **Vocabulary bank** Complete the sentences with the correct form of the words in parentheses.

1 I love movies with a lot of _____action_____ . (act)

2 That's a bad cut. I think you might need medical _____ . (treat)

3 I wonder what kind of _____ we'll get this time. (punish)

4 What a great _____! Let's go right now. (suggest)

5 Will I get an _____ to your party? (invite)

6 Looking directly at the sun can cause _____ . (blind)

7 You need a lot of _____ to write a good sitcom. (create)

8 Let me show you this great job _____ . (advertise)

9 It's complete _____ to think you can pass the exams without studying. (mad)

3 Pronunciation

✱ Word stress

a ▶ CD3 T30 Listen and <u>underline</u> the stressed syllables. In which pairs of words does the stress change?

1 pre<u>pare</u>   prepa<u>ra</u>tion
2 prefer   preference
3 enjoy   enjoyment
4 lazy   laziness
5 protect   protection
6 popular   popularity

b Practice saying each pair of words.

4 Grammar

✱ Verbs with gerunds or infinitives

a Match the sentences with the pictures. Write A–D in the boxes.

1 I stopped to take a look at the map.   `B`

2 I remember mailing the letter.   ☐

3 I remembered to mail the letter.   ☐

4 I stopped looking at the map.   ☐

b Match the questions and the answers.

1 Did you remember to call Jane?
2 Don't you remember telling that joke before?
3 Why are you so late?
4 Do you want a hamburger?
5 When are you going to stop playing that game?

a No, thanks. I stopped eating meat.
b I'm on the last level. Almost done!
c No, I'll give her a call now.
d I stopped to buy you some flowers.
e Oh, I'm sorry. Well, it's still funny.

c (Circle) the correct words. Sometimes there is more than one possibility.

1 It's started (to snow) / (snowing.) Snowball fight!

2 I remember to see / seeing that girl at Rachel's party. Who is she?

3 I hate to watch / watching romantic movies.

4 I stopped to eat / eating chicken years ago.

5 I stopped to buy / buying a CD on my way home.

6 She loves to go / going to the movies on Saturday afternoons.

7 Did you remember to tell / telling Owen where we're meeting tonight? I hope you didn't forget.

8 They began to work / working on the road at 6:00 a.m. Can you believe it?

Fiction in mind

a Read more from "Water of Wanting" by Frank Brennan. What happened to the two sets of laboratory mice? What do you think the water contains?

Jean Pascal put a small drop of clear liquid into the drinking water of his mice.

¹_____ But Jean soon noticed that when there was the liquid in the water, they came back to drink it more than usual. They couldn't have been thirsty anymore, but they drank. He needed to check this carefully.

Jean was now a brilliant chemist. He worked in Montreal, Canada, for a large chemical company. His company made a lot of different chemicals, including chemicals for food, which are often called additives. Additives give food a different color or flavor or even make it last longer. ²_____

The mice kept coming back for more water. Their stomachs were already completely full of liquid, but they still wanted to drink more. They just couldn't get enough of the water that had Jean's additive

in it. They didn't want to eat any food at all. ³_____ And, amazingly, they were still trying to reach the water as they were dying.

He cut the amount of WOW that he added to his mice's water by half. ⁴_____ Then he added much smaller amounts of WOW: The mice drank less, but they still came back for little drinks of water all the time. These little drinks were still far more than the mice needed. It was as if they had become addicted to water. They weren't interested in anything else. They didn't even want food. This time they didn't die of too much water. They all died of hunger.

(from Brennan, F. [2009] "Water of Wanting" in *Tasty Tales*, CUP: pp. 4–6)

Tasty Tales
Frank Brennan

b Read the extract again and put one of the following sentences in each space. There is one sentence you won't need.

A Food companies pay a lot of money for additives that work well.

B Normally, the mice drank only when they were thirsty.

C Soon they died because their tiny bodies were too full of water.

D It was big and expensive, and it exploded in his face.

E The results were the same.

c Choose the correct way to complete the statements, according to the text.

1 In his first experiment, Jean observed that
   a the mice were eating more than usual.
   b the liquid affected the mice's thirst.
   c the mice died almost immediately.
   d he had put too much liquid into the water.

2 Food additives
   a can keep food fresh longer.
   b are mostly manufactured in Canada.
   c are natural parts of most food.
   d do not change the way something tastes.

3 The first group of mice
   a drank all the water at once.
   b finally became satisfied and stopped drinking.
   c ate too much and couldn't drink any more water.
   d didn't realize the water was killing them.

4 In the second experiment,
   a the WOW concentration was doubled.
   b the mice still drank more than was necessary.
   c the mice drank even more than before.
   d the mice died the same way as in the first experiment.

Skills in mind

6 Listen

a ▶ CD3 T31 You will hear part of an interview with a movie critic about how monsters have changed in movies. Listen and check (✔) the characters he mentions.

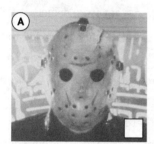
Friday the 13th: Jason

Frankenstein: Frankenstein's Monster

Dracula

Nightmare on Elm Street: Freddy

b ▶ CD3 T31 Listen again and complete the sentences.

1 People have always been fascinated by monsters and the dark side ....

2 Without bad there is no such thing ....

3 The late .... and the early part of the .... was the golden age of the monster.

4 Frankenstein's monster and Mr. Hyde were the results of humans trying to ....

5 .... have no motivation. They're very two-dimensional.

6 Freddy, Jason and Michael Myers are really just three ....

7 Audiences just want to see how many ....

8 All these monsters do is make us scared to go to ....

LISTENING TIP

How to complete sentences

- As with all listening exercises, read through the questions carefully before you listen. This will help prepare you for what you might expect to hear.

- Try to predict what the missing word(s) might be. However, remember that your predictions may be wrong, so you still need to listen carefully to check.

- You will not always hear the exact words that are in the question. Listen carefully for different words that are used that have the same meaning.

  For example, question 1 says:

  People have always been *fascinated by* monsters.

  You heard:

  The human race has always been *extremely interested in* monsters.

- You are usually only expected to write between one and three words. No more.

- Finally, read through your answers carefully. Make sure they are grammatically correct and check your spelling.

Unit check

1 Fill in the blanks

Complete the text with the words in the box.

> getting   to get   to play   imagination
> characters   strategy   ~~entertainment~~
> graphics   playing   popularity

The best form of __entertainment__ for me is a good computer game. One with cool ¹_____ that seem like real people. And it has to have good ²_____ , so that you feel like you're right there in the action. I don't like games that are too simple. I like trying to figure out the ³_____ of the game. You know, I enjoy ⁴_____ into the mind of the game's creator. The best games need a lot of ⁵_____ , because there are so many boring games out there. The ⁶_____ of a game doesn't really matter to me just because everyone wants ⁷_____ it doesn't mean it's good. I actually don't mind ⁸_____ older games. I'd love ⁹_____ the original PacMan one day. It's amazing!

| | 9 |

2 Choose the correct answers

(Circle) the correct answer: a, b or c.

1 Steven Spielberg has such a fantastic _____ .
  a imagine   b imaginity   c (imagination)

2 I must remember _____ the DVD back to the store today.
  a taking   b to take   c take

3 I like a computer game that _____ me and makes me think.
  a challenges   b strategies   c controls

4 That teacher is well known for her _____ .
  a kind   b kindly   c kindness

5 You should _____ drinking too much soda. It's not good for you.
  a choose   b avoid   c afford

6 They don't feel like _____ to the party tonight.
  a going   b to going   c to go

7 My parents don't _____ about anything.
  a agree   b agreement   c agreeing

8 After walking six kilometers, they stopped _____ a drink.
  a to have   b having   c have

9 I suggested _____ a cheaper phone, but he didn't listen.
  a buy   b you to buy   c buying

| | 8 |

3 Vocabulary

Complete the sentences with nouns made from the underlined words.

1 He thinks it's <u>possible</u>, but I don't see any __possibility__ of it happening.

2 Are they <u>different</u>? I can't see any _____ between them.

3 So what if he's <u>popular</u>! I don't care about _____ .

4 Did you say you want me to <u>protect</u> you? Why do you need _____ ?

5 You're so <u>creative</u>! I wish I had your _____ .

6 Please don't <u>punish</u> me. I can't stand _____ .

7 A: Did you <u>enjoy</u> the game?
  B: It wasn't what I'd call _____ .

8 I've been <u>preparing</u> for this all week. That's enough _____ .

9 She <u>reacted</u> badly. In fact, I was really surprised at her _____ .

| | 8 |

How did you do?

Total: | | 25

| :) Very good 25 – 20 | :\| OK 19 – 16 | :(Review Unit 9 again 15 or less |

Be honest!

1 Grammar

✱ Second conditional review

a Match the sentences with the pictures. Write 1–6 in the boxes.

1 If we win the World Cup, it will be the best day of my life.

2 If I had my shorts, I would play soccer.

3 If the rain doesn't stop tomorrow, we won't be able to have a barbecue.

4 If it rained tomorrow, I would be very happy.

5 If you are 18, you can come in.

6 If you were 18, you could come in.

A

B

C

D

E

F
1

b Complete the text. Use the correct form of the verbs in parentheses and *would*, *'d*, *wouldn't* or *might*.

Imagine I ___*found*___ (find) $100 in the street. I'm not sure what I ___*'d do*___ (do). If I ¹_____ (take) it to the police station, they ²_____ (not be) interested. If I ³_____ (ask) in the nearest store, the salesperson ⁴_____ (say) it was hers. If I ⁵_____ (give) it to my sister, I'm sure she ⁶_____ (spend) it on clothes. If I ⁷_____ (tell) my friends, they ⁸_____ (want) to spend it, and if I ⁹_____ (keep) it, I ¹⁰_____ (feel) guilty. I hope I never find $100 in the street!

c Put the words in order to make the sentences.

1 your / asked / friend / Say / you / best / shoplift / to

Say your best friend asked you to shoplift.

2 you / fighting / the / saw / Imagine / two / street / men / in

_____

3 forgot / really / test / Suppose / to / for / study / a / you / important

_____

4 in / found / you / restaurant / Say / $500 / a

_____

5 if / borrowed / friend's / and / it / you / What / broke / your / stereo ?

_____

d Write your own answers to the questions in Exercise 1c. What would you do?

1 *I'd tell him I thought it was wrong.*

2 ....
....

3 ....
....

4 ....
....

5 ....

2 Vocabulary

✴ Crimes

a Read the descriptions of the crimes and write the names of the crimes in the blanks. Choose from the words in the box.

> burglary joyriding arson
> shoplifting pick-pocketing
> ~~vandalism~~

1 Have you seen the school?
They've sprayed graffiti all over it.
___*vandalism*___

2 They broke a window to get in, but they only took the TV and the DVD player. ....

3 When he was only 12, he broke into a car and drove it around, just for fun. ....

4 I was on the bus. I felt a hand, and when I looked for my wallet it was gone. ....

5 The police are treating the fire at the school as suspicious.

....

6 When she was at the mall, she took some clothes without paying for them. ....

✴ Crime verbs

b Complete the sentences with the words in the box.

> caught wrong into law ~~away~~ crime

1 Sixteen-year-old John's been getting ___*away*___ with shoplifting for two years until last week when he got .... with 10 CDs hidden in his coat.

2 When Steve was a teenager, he was always getting .... trouble with the police for vandalism, shoplifting and things like that. Now he's 25, and he's committed a more serious .... – arson. He burned the town library down.

3 Helen knew she was doing something .... She knew that going at 80 mph was breaking the .... , but she didn't think she would have an accident. She's OK, but four innocent people are in the hospital with serious injuries.

c What punishment do you think each of the people in Exercise 2b should get? Choose from the words in the box.

> pay a fine be put on probation
> do community service be sent to prison

1 *John should do 30 hours of community service and be put on probation.*

2 ....

3 ....

Vocabulary bank Match the words 1–8 with their definitions. Write a–h in the boxes.

1	murderer	c	a	a person who attacks someone in the street and takes their valuables
2	assassin		b	the act of killing another person
3	mugger		c	a person who kills another person or people
4	break-in		d	someone who steals things
5	murder		e	the act of taking things that do not belong to you
6	mug		f	the act of entering someone's house illegally, usually by breaking a window
7	thief		g	someone who deliberately kills a well-known person
8	theft		h	to attack someone and take things from them

3 Grammar

✶ I wish / if only

a Circle the correct words.

1 I wish I (*were*) / *was* a little thinner.

2 If only I *could* / *can* go to the party tonight.

3 My sister wishes she *has* / *had* a boyfriend.

4 Darren wishes he *didn't* / *doesn't* spend so much time playing computer games.

5 My dad wishes he *weren't* / *isn't* so busy.

6 If only she *loves* / *loved* me.

7 I wish I *don't* / *didn't* have so much homework.

8 If only I *know* / *knew* the answer.

b Mike isn't happy. Read what he says and write *I wish / if only* sentences.

1 "I can't drive, and I don't have a car."

   He wishes he could drive, and he wishes he had a car.

2 "My parents don't understand me."

   ....

3 "My little brother annoys me all the time."

   ....

4 "My computer's broken."

   ....

5 "I don't have enough money to buy a new bike."

   ....

6 "I can't find my house keys."

   ....

7 "I'm too shy to talk to girls."

   ....

c Look at the pictures and write *I wish / if only* sentences for each of the people.

1 *If only I weren't so hungry.*   2 ....   3 ....

4 ....   5 ....   6 ....

7 ....   8 ....   9 ....

4 Pronunciation

★ *I wish ...* and *if only ...*

▶ **CD3 T32** Listen and repeat. Pay attention to the stress of *If only* and *I wish*.

1 I wish I were somewhere else.

2 If only he loved me.

3 I wish I didn't have so many problems.

4 If only I could go to the party.

5 I wish it were Saturday.

6 If only she understood.

5 Listen

Use the words from the song "I Wish" to complete the sentences. Check with the song on page 68 of the Student's Book.

> scene   hang around   ~~freeze~~   twist   breeze   turned into

1 You'll _____*freeze*_____ if you go out without a coat. It's snowing.

2 It was a perfect day on the beach. It was a nice, sunny day with a gentle _____ to keep you cool.

3 There was this really scary scene in the movie. The man started to _____ and turn until he _____ this terrible monster, half man and half wolf.

4 My grandfather was part of the music _____ in Liverpool in the 1960s. He says he used to _____ with the Beatles, but I'm not sure if I believe that.

6 Study help

★ Key word transformations

In this type of exercise you have to rewrite a sentence using a given word so that it means the same thing. For example:

John is interested in knowing more about astronomy. LIKE

John _____ know more about astronomy.

- Think carefully about the key word. How does this relate to the sentence? For example, *is interested in* can have a similar meaning to *would like*.

- Is the key word part of a phrasal verb? Is it part of an idiom?

- Identify and underline the part of the sentence you need to change. For example, *is interested in knowing*.

- What else do you need to know about the key word? For example, *would like* is followed by the infinitive.

- Think carefully about the tense. Usually both sentences will be in the same tense, but be careful with words like *wish* and conditionals when the tense may change.

- Always check your answer carefully for basic mistakes.

Skills in mind

Write

a Read the essay and put the paragraphs in the correct order. Write 1–4 in the boxes.

"There would be less crime on the streets if there were more after-school programs for teenagers." Discuss this statement and give your own opinion.

A. Schools and community centers should provide more programs to help reduce teen violence. Teenagers would have organized activities they enjoy that are supervised by adults. If there were more activities to do after school, crime rates would decrease. Teenagers would have places to be, and they would not be on the streets. ☐

B. I believe the answer to solving the problem of teenage violence is education. There need to be programs for teenagers so they have things to do to stay out of trouble, but their parents also need to be educated. If teenagers also had support at home, teen crimes might decrease. ☐

C. Unfortunately, this will not solve all of the problems with teen crime. It would be difficult to get some teenagers interested in the programs. They could choose not to go. Older brothers and sisters also influence many teens. Even if more programs started today, many teenagers would still be around violence in their communities. ☐

D. Approximately 15 percent of people arrested in the United States each year are teenagers. Some of the crimes are minor, but they also commit violent crimes. Research shows that many of these crimes happen after 3:00 p.m. when teenagers are not at school. When some teenagers aren't supervised and don't have planned activities to do after school, they turn to crime. ☐

b Match the paragraphs with the summaries 1–4. Write A–D in the boxes.

1 Arguments that agree with the title ☐

2 An introduction ☐

3 The writer's opinion ☐

4 Arguments that disagree with the title ☐

WRITING TIP

Developing a discursive essay (1)

- A useful way to organize discursive essays is in four paragraphs:
  1 introduction
  2 arguments for or against
  3 arguments against or for
  4 your opinion

- Read the statement carefully and decide what your opinion is. Make notes to support your argument.

- Make notes under two headings: *for* and *against*. Use these for your second and third paragraphs.

- Good ways to start an essay are:
  – Statistics: "Approximately 15 percent of people arrested in the United States ... "
  – A question to be answered: "How can after-school programs reduce crime?"
  – A sentence supporting the statement: "There is too much teen crime ... "

c Write an essay of about 250 words about this statement:

"The world would be a better place if people under 40 made the decisions." Discuss.

Unit check

1 Fill in the blanks

Complete the text with the words in the box.

> would   imagine   caught   crime   put
> away   can   ~~wish~~   could   into

You have an important composition for your history class in the morning. It's 10 p.m. You _____wish_____ you had started earlier, and it's really beginning to get you down. Well, ¹_____ you ²_____ pay 20 dollars to have it done for you and get an A? What ³_____ you do? Cheating via the Internet is a serious problem for many schools and universities, and many students are getting ⁴_____ with it. For a small price, students ⁵_____ buy work from one of many websites. However, if students get ⁶_____ , they can get ⁷_____ serious trouble. It is a ⁸_____ to pay someone to do your homework. Most schools will ⁹_____ students on probation, and many will even expel them.

| 9 |

2 Choose the correct answers

Circle the correct answer: a, b or c.

1 He _____ the job down because the money wasn't very good.
   a talked   b played   c (turned)

2 If I _____ your help, I would ask you for it.
   a needed   b need   c will need

3 Nobody saw us. I think we've gotten _____ with it.
   a away   b over   c up

4 I was driving too fast, and now I have to _____ a fine.
   a do   b pay   c spend

5 My little brother's always _____ into trouble with my parents.
   a being   b going   c getting

6 They broke _____ my house, but they didn't take anything.
   a into   b up   c over

7 They made him _____ 100 hours of community service for vandalizing the old factory.
   a spend   b make   c do

8 If only I _____ have so many problems.
   a didn't   b don't   c not

9 You might go to prison if you _____ the law.
   a do   b make   c break

| 8 |

How did you do?

Total: | 25 |

3 Vocabulary

Use the words in parentheses to form a word that fits in the blank.

These days more young people are _____breaking_____ (BREAK) the law than ever. There are more adolescent ¹_____ (CRIME) than ever before. But it isn't all bad news. On the whole, young people aren't ²_____ (COMMIT) what are considered serious crimes like murder. However, they often do things like going into some stores and ³_____ (SHOP), i.e., taking goods without paying. Another more common crime for young people is to steal cars. They take the cars and go ⁴_____ (JOYRIDE). It often ends in disaster as they frequently end up crashing the cars. Sadly, many young people are found guilty of ⁵_____ (VANDAL), and they often can't even explain why they did the damage in the first place. Luckily, there are not too many young ⁶_____ (ARSON), which is a good thing. But for young criminals, there is no point in ⁷_____ (SEND) them to prison. One of the better options is to give them some hours of ⁸_____ (COMMUNE) service. That way they pay back the people they live with.

| 8 |

| ☺ Very good 25 – 20 | ☹ OK 19 – 16 | ☹ Review Unit 10 again 15 or less |

The truth is out there!

1 Grammar

✱ Linkers of contrast: *however / although / despite / even though / in spite of*

a Complete the sentences with the words in the box.

> didn't go   didn't buy   bought   ~~went~~   don't feel like   feel like

1 Although I wasn't feeling very well, I __went__ to school.

2 Despite the fact it was expensive, I _____ it.

3 Even though it's my birthday, I _____ celebrating.

4 In spite of the fact the sun was shining, we _____ on a picnic.

5 I know it's only 9 p.m. However, I _____ going to bed.

6 Even though they're my favorite band, I _____ their new CD.

b Look at the pictures. (Circle) the correct words.

1 The place looks beautiful. *In spite of /* (*However,*) I couldn't live there.

2 *Although / Despite* I usually love horror movies, *Scream* was too scary for me.

3 So you haven't done any work, *even though / in spite of* your exams start tomorrow?

4 *Although / However* I can't speak English very well, I can understand American movies fine.

5 We had a great vacation *although / in spite of* the rain.

①

②

③

④

⑤

c Rewrite the sentences. Use the words in parentheses.

1 Although she doesn't like rock music, she went to the concert. (despite)

She went to the concert, despite the fact that she doesn't like rock music.

2 We could understand him, even though his accent was very strong. (in spite of)

_____
_____
_____

3 Despite not being very hungry, I ate two pieces of cake. (although)

_____
_____
_____

4 The main course was delicious, but the dessert was a little disappointing. (however)

_____
_____
_____

5 Even though he's not very tall, he plays basketball really well. (despite)

_____
_____
_____

2 Pronunciation

✱ /oʊ/ *though*

▶ **CD3 T33** Listen and repeat. Pay attention to the sound /oʊ/.

1 Nobody knows except Joe.
2 Don't drive so slowly in the snow.
3 Even though she didn't go, I enjoyed the show.
4 Although she won't tell me, I already know.

3 Vocabulary

✱ Problems

a Complete the sentences with the prepositions in the box.

> up   away   over   on   up   out
> over   ~~up~~   back

1 I'll be home late tonight. A problem has *come* __up__ at work.

2 If you have a problem at school, why don't you *talk it* _____ with your teacher?

3 I can't *make* _____ *my mind* about what to wear tonight.

4 Don't worry about it. I'm sure it'll *go* _____ by itself.

5 I can't give you a decision now. Can I have a few minutes to *think it* _____?

6 When nobody knows what to do, Dan always *comes* _____ *with* a great idea.

7 Why don't you *sleep* _____ *it* and give me an answer tomorrow?

8 That's a good point, but I'd like to *come* _____ to it a little later.

9 Let's try to *sort* _____ who is doing what before we start.

b Complete the text with the correct form of the expressions in *italics* in Exercise 3a.

The problem ____*came up*____ (appeared) really unexpectedly. It was a simple question, but I couldn't ¹_____ (suggest) an answer.

I wanted some time to ²_____ (keep it in my mind), but I had to ³_____ (decide) quickly. It wasn't the sort of problem you needed to ⁴_____ (take more time), and there were people waiting behind me.

Maybe I could ⁵_____ (discuss it) with the cashier? No, she didn't look very interested.

This was one problem that wasn't going to ⁶_____ (disappear) by itself. And I couldn't ⁷_____ (return) to it later. I had to ⁸_____ (find a solution) now. And then she asked me again, "Would you like French fries or onion rings with your hamburger?"

c **Vocabulary bank** (Circle) the correct words.

1 We need some good advice on how to (deal with)/ *share* this problem.

2 Will it *cause / invent* a problem if I leave class early today?

3 Let's hope we can do this without *walking / running* into too many problems.

4 Deciding on the best way to start my presentation tomorrow is turning into a real *headache / drawback*.

5 My young brother's teachers say that he's behaving like a *potential / problem* child these days.

6 Thanks for your help. It would have been a *major / minor* problem if you hadn't been there.

7 Let's try and *jump / overcome* the problem together.

8 The trip sounds great, but not having a car will be a *solution / drawback*.

4 Grammar

✱ Modal verbs of deduction (present)

a Match the two sentences. Write a–f in the boxes.

1 He can't be hungry. | d | a She's his best friend!
2 He must be hungry. | | b He didn't have a very big lunch.
3 He might be hungry. | | c He doesn't have a phone!
4 She must know his phone number. | | d He's just eaten two large pizzas!
5 She can't know his phone number. | | e She's a friend of his sister's.
6 She might know his phone number. | | f He hasn't eaten for 48 hours!

b Rewrite the sentences so they mean the opposite.

1 It might not be true.
It might be true.

2 She must be happy.
....

3 They might speak English.
....

4 You can't like olives!
....

5 They might not know.
....

6 He must live near here.
....

c Complete the sentences with *must*, *can't* or *might*.

1 That pan has just come out of the oven. It
...*must*... be hot.

2 They're speaking Spanish, and I think they're from South America. They .... be from Peru.

3 She .... know. It's a secret!

4 I'm not sure what it is. It .... be some kind of monkey.

5 Everyone passes that exam. It .... be very difficult.

6 That bird's eating the bananas. It ....
like them!

d Write sentences about the pictures. Use *can't* and *must*.

1 Her boyfriend sends her flowers every day.
He must love her a lot.

2 They've been walking for two days. They ....
....

3 Hardly anyone came to see them. They ....
....

4 They decided not to go to the movie. It ....

5 There were cameras everywhere. She ....

6 He spent another birthday on his own. He ....

5 Culture in mind

New Animals

In northern Vietnam, in thick forests in the North Annamite Mountains, there is a wildlife park called Vu Quang. In 1986, the area was made an official forest reserve. In 2002, 550 square kilometers of the area were declared a national park. Vu Quang is not an ordinary park, though. For one thing, it's in an area that is hard to get to. And it's an area that's difficult to walk through because the rocks are covered with algae and are very slippery. But that's not all that is unusual about Vu Quang. In the last 20 years, several species of animals that have never been seen anywhere in the world before have been discovered there. Some of them have just been discovered, so scientists haven't even given them official names yet.

The animals discovered at the park include five species of fish, two species of amphibians and fifteen species of reptiles. Several species of deer have also been found there. The biggest discovery in the reserve is the Vu Quang ox or saola.

The saola is the largest animal discovered on land in over 100 years, so it causes a lot of excitement in the scientific world. It looks like it is related to antelope or cattle, but it has many unusual characteristics. Its fur is a reddish brown, and it has many white spots and stripes. It has white stripes above its eyes that look like eyebrows. Its horns are very smooth and can be one to two feet long — twice the size of its head! In fact, the name "saola" is a word that describes its horns in the local language.

The saola had hidden safely for years in the Vu Quang area. But once it was discovered, it was in danger. Some hunters have no respect for the new species. Sadly, the saola is an endangered species.

a Choose the correct answer: a, b, c or d.

1 Between 1986 and 2002, the Vu Quang area was
   a a national park.
   b a mountain.
   c a wildlife reserve.
   d a forest reserve.

2 It wouldn't be a good idea to go hiking in the area because
   a there are too many rocks.
   b it's cold and rains a lot.
   c it's slippery underfoot.
   d it's easy to get lost.

3 Some of the new species discovered
   a don't have official names.
   b are birds.
   c have been seen in other places in the world.
   d were discovered somewhere else first.

4 The saola is an important discovery because
   a it's the largest deer in the world.
   b it's the largest mammal discovered on land in over 100 years.
   c it's the largest antelope ever discovered.
   d it's the newest species of cattle.

5 The saola is a word that describes the animal's
   a eyebrows.
   b fur.
   c head.
   d horns.

6 The saola is now
   a being hunted and endangered.
   b increasing in number.
   c hidden from people and other animals.
   d no longer in the Vu Quang area.

b Match the words 1–6 with their definitions. Write a–f in the boxes.

1 official   d
2 algae
3 slippery
4 characteristic
5 local
6 respect

a green plants that grow on rocks in water
b something that is typical of a person or thing
c admiration and appreciation
d connected with authority
e causing things to slip and slide because it is wet
f existing in a particular place

UNIT 11   65

6 Read

Read the movie review of *The Lake* and choose from the list (A–G) the phrase that best summarized each part (1–6) of the review. There is one extra phrase you won't need.

A A nurse meets a hero

B The actors and a young star

C A nurse returns home

D One disappointment

E A suspenseful story

F A nice surprise

G Aliens take over

READING TIP

Matching summaries with paragraphs

- First of all, do not look at the summary phrases to start with. Read the text completely first.

- Think of your own short summary of each part of the text.

- Now read the summary phrases. Do any match your own summaries? Write in the answers.

- Look at the remaining summary phrases carefully. Try and match vocabulary in them to vocabulary in the passage.

- Finally, never leave an answer space empty. If you really have no idea, try to guess.

Movie review: *The Lake* (1998)

1

Yasmine Bleeth is Jackie Ivers, a Los Angeles nurse who moves back to her hometown, San Vicente, California. She soon notices that her friends and family are acting strangely. She realizes that everyone who goes into the town's lake comes out acting differently.

2

Jackie figures out what is going on. Aliens live on another planet. It is like Earth, but it is extremely polluted, so the aliens can't live there much longer. They are planning to replace people on Earth, and they enter Earth through the lake. When someone goes into the lake, an alien takes over that person's body.

3

The Lake is an entertaining science fiction movie. It's a movie that was made for TV, and it is surprisingly good for a TV movie. There is plenty of action to keep viewers on the edge of their seats.

4

Perhaps the reason for this is the strength of the director, David Jackson. He really understands what a science fiction movie is and creates a tense storyline with suspense in the movie from beginning to end.

5

Yasmine Bleeth's performance is OK as the nurse and main character of the story. The other actors are also all right, including Marion Ross. After watching her for years as the mother on the TV show *Happy Days*, it was enjoyable to see her perform in a different genre. But the best performance of the movie is from Haley Joel Osment. He was only 10 years old at the time. He later became famous when he starred in the movie *The Sixth Sense* with Bruce Willis.

6

My only criticism is that some of the characters are slow to figure out what is going on. It's disappointing because it makes the characters not very believable. The viewer figures out the truth long before the characters do. It made me wonder, "What's wrong with these people? Why couldn't they figure *that* out?" But overall, it is a good movie, and it's worth seeing.

Unit check

1 Fill in the blanks

Complete the text with the words in the box.

| result   came up   go away   minds   image   ~~might~~   although   coming back   sort   ignore |

From the death of Lady Diana to the UFO crash at Roswell, everybody loves a good mystery. They love guessing who _____*might*_____ be the killer or what happened. [1]_____ most of us forget them quickly, there are some people who dedicate their lives to them. As a [2]_____ there are now hundreds of web pages about unsolved mysteries, and people try to [3]_____ them out.

Some unsolved mysteries won't [4]_____ , and they just keep [5]_____ . The [6]_____ of President John F. Kennedy's assassination is one many people remember. A survey done in 2003 to mark the 40th anniversary of JFK's death [7]_____ with the amazing statistic that 74 percent of Americans don't believe that Lee Harvey Oswald was the assassin. American people have made up their [8]_____ , and they choose to [9]_____ what the government says. They have their own ideas about who assassinated JFK.

9

2 Choose the correct answers

Circle the correct answer: a, b or c.

1 Although _____ the theme park, I don't want to go there again.
   a I liking   b liking   c (I liked)

2 Should I buy the red dress or blue one? I can't _____ up my mind.
   a make   b decide   c do

3 It's not so serious. I'm sure we can _____ it out.
   a make   b sort   c think

4 I decided to travel by train, _____ it was more expensive than the bus.
   a despite   b even though   c however

5 It's boiling today. It _____ be at least 35°C.
   a might   b must   c can't

6 I have a problem, and I want to _____ it over with you.
   a say   b talk   c speak

7 _____ knowing a lot about computers, she couldn't solve the problem.
   a Despite   b However   c Although

8 Why don't you _____ on it and make a decision in the morning?
   a sleep   b relax   c lie

9 She didn't go to my party. She _____ like me very much.
   a can't   b must   c might

8

3 Vocabulary

Complete the text. Write one word in each space.

I was working on my go-kart the other day when I _____*ran*_____ into a few problems. I wasn't sure how to [1]_____ with them, but Dad said he would help and that we would be able to [2]_____ them out. He sat down for a few minutes to [3]_____ it over, and then he [4]_____ up with an answer. "I know what's [5]_____ the problem," he said. "And I'm sure we can [6]_____ it together!" And sure enough, after 15 minutes, my go-kart was working again. My dad's like that. When he [7]_____ up his mind to do something, he does it! Of course, I said thanks for his help. He made a [8]_____ seem easy!

8

How did you do?

Total: **25**

| ☺ | Very good 25 – 20 | ☺ | OK 19 – 16 | ☹ | Review Unit 11 again 15 or less |

12 Mysterious places

1 Grammar
✱ Modals of deduction (past)

a (Circle) the correct words.

1 She must have left because her car is *still here / not here.*
2 They couldn't have played well because they *lost / won.*
3 He might have lost my number because he *called / didn't call* me.
4 You couldn't have seen my brother because I *have / don't have* any brothers!
5 We must have done something wrong because he looks really *angry / happy.*
6 I couldn't have eaten your chicken sandwich because I *eat / don't eat* meat.

b Complete the dialogue about the objects in the photo with the words in the box.

> couldn't have built   might be   could have built   must weigh   could have been
> don't believe   must have been   ~~might have used~~

Sally: Wow, look at those. They're amazing.
What do you think they were used for?

Mike: The guidebook says that nobody's sure,
but the people here *might have used* them
to honor important people on the island.

Sally: I think they ¹_____ images of leaders
that the island people worshipped.

Mike: You ²_____ right.

Sally: Do you think that aliens
³_____ them?

Mike: No, I ⁴_____ that.

Sally: But humans ⁵_____ them.
Each statue ⁶_____ hundreds
of kilograms.

Mike: But they did build them. Our ancestors
⁷_____ more intelligent than we think!

c Complete the sentences with *must*, *might* or *could* and the verb.

1 The exam *must have been* (be) very difficult.
Only one person passed.

2 He _____ (leave) the country.
He doesn't have a passport.

3 Our dog didn't come home last night. I'm
worried a car _____ (run) him over.

4 You _____ (finish) that book!
You just bought it yesterday.

5 She _____ (be) really hungry. Did you
see how much she ate?

6 I think I _____ (see) this movie before,
but I can't remember.

d Complete the sentences with your own ideas.

1 I can't find my wallet. I think I might _____ *have left it in a store* _____ .
2 Jane looks really excited. She must _____ .
3 Did he really say that? He must _____ .
4 This band is terrible. They couldn't _____ .
5 She's a half an hour late. I think she might _____ .
6 He never bought her a present in 10 years of marriage. He couldn't _____ .
7 Nobody came to his party. He must _____ .
8 I'm not sure how he crashed the car. He might _____ .

2 Pronunciation

✱ *have* in *must have / might have / couldn't have*

a ▶ CD3 T34 Listen and complete the sentences.

1 They _____ been disappointed.
2 She _____ left already.
3 I _____ helped you.

4 She _____ gone home.
5 We _____ forgotten to tell him.
6 She _____ seen us.

b ▶ CD3 T34 Listen again and repeat the sentences.

3 Grammar

✱ Indirect questions with *be*

a Circle the correct words.

1 I wonder how old *he is* / *is he*.
2 How old *he is* / *is he*?
3 I can't tell you where *they're* / *are they* from.
4 Where *they're* / *are they* from?

5 I don't understand why *he's* / *is he* unhappy.
6 Why *he's* / *is he* unhappy?
7 I don't know what *we're* / *are we* going to do.
8 What *we're* / *are we* going to do?

b Look at the pictures and complete the sentences.

1 She's wondering _____ *who he was* _____ .

2 They're not sure _____
   _____ .

3 He doesn't know _____
   _____ .

4 He doesn't understand _____
   _____ .

5 She won't tell him _____
   _____ .

6 She wonders _____
   _____ .

✴ **Indirect questions in the simple present and past**

c Finish the sentences with a period (.) or a question mark (?).

1 They wanted to know when the train left ......
2 Why do you walk so quickly ......
3 Do you know what I think ......
4 Where did you park your car ......

5 He wondered why she didn't talk to him ......
6 I don't know where they are ......
7 What time does the store open ......
8 Can you tell me what language she speaks ......

d Complete the questions with the words in the box.

> did she speak to   she spoke to   ~~they live~~
> do you drive to school   the movie starts
> do they live   you drive to school
> does the movie start

1 Can you tell me where _____*they live*_____ ?
2 Where _____ ?
3 When _____ ?
4 Do you know when _____ ?
5 Who _____ ?
6 Do you happen to know who
   _____ ?
7 How far _____ ?
8 Can you tell me how far _____ ?

e Put the words in the correct order to make questions.

1 need / visa / tell / Can / you / me / I / if / a
   Can you tell me if I need a visa?

2 need / I / visa / Do / a
   _____ ?

3 went / know / you / Do / they / where
   _____ ?

4 did / they / go / Where
   _____ ?

5 left / Brazil / you / they / when / Do / know / for
   _____ ?

6 Brazil / When / for / did / they / leave
   _____ ?

4 Vocabulary

✴ **Phrasal verbs**

a Match the two parts of the sentences. Write a–f in the boxes.

1 He's the managing director now, but he started ☐ c
2 Her hard work paid ☐
3 She's unhappy because her cat passed ☐
4 I was kind of scared when the lights went ☐
5 We didn't have enough players so we had to call ☐
6 He doesn't really like musicals, but we managed to talk ☐

a   him into going with us.
b   out because it was really dark.
c   out as an assistant.
d   off, and she won the race.
e   off the soccer game.
f   away yesterday.

b Replace the underlined words with the phrasal verbs in the box.

> ~~came across~~   passed away   called off   went out   tied in with

1 I was reading an old book, and I <u>found</u> my first boyfriend's phone number written in it. *came across*
2 The police are sure he's <u>connected with</u> the robbery. _____
3 They've <u>canceled</u> the school party because nobody's interested in it. _____
4 My grandfather <u>died</u> peacefully in his sleep. _____
5 We didn't have any more wood, and the fire <u>stopped burning</u>. _____

c   Complete the crossword.

1 We arrived really late because Helen's car _broke_ down.

2 I hadn't seen Jim for years, but I _____ into him yesterday by chance.

3 It's a personal thing, so I don't feel like _____ into it right now, OK?

4 When we were in Japan, we _____ up some old friends of my parents.

5 I hate it when you put me _____ in front of our friends.

6 I have so much homework to do! It's starting to _____ me down.

7 Thanks for inviting me, but I'm afraid I'll have to _____ the invitation down.

8 All the hotels were full, but luckily our friends put us _____ for the night.

9 Experts are looking _____ last week's train crash, to try to find out what caused it.

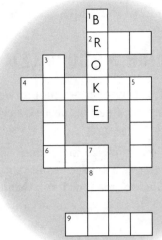

d Complete the sentences with the correct prepositions.

1 Don't worry about looking for that pen. I'm sure it'll turn _up_ somewhere.

2 Look, I hate sports, so there's no way you can talk me _____ playing tennis tomorrow!

3 It's a great movie. It starts as a thriller, but after about 15 minutes, it turns _____ a comedy!

4 I was on the Internet for hours, and then suddenly I came _____ something really interesting.

5 I'm afraid my sister's sick, so we have to call _____ tomorrow night's party.

6 I asked Sue Jones to go out with me next weekend, but she turned me _____ .

7 A lot of us were late for school today because the school bus broke _____ !

8 I had to give _____ dance classes because I don't have enough time.

5 Everyday English

Circle the correct words.

1 **A:** I hope I never see Marco again!
   B: Well, look *up / out* because here he comes now!

2 **A:** Can you give this to Mary, please?
   B: Sure. I'll give it to her the *time / moment* she gets here.

3 **A:** What? Muse is coming to play in our town next year?!
   B: No, of course not! *Just / Not* kidding, Maria.

4 **A:** My dad was really angry when I got home last night.
   B: Serves you *left / right*! If you come home at 3 in the morning, what do you expect?

5 **A:** I'm really sorry that I'm late.
   B: Don't worry about it! Ten minutes doesn't matter. *Besides / However*, it's not your fault that the train was late.

6 **A:** So tell me what Tom said.
   B: No! It's none of your *things / business*! If you really want to know, go and ask Tom.

6 Write a story (1)

a Mark's teacher asked him to write a story ending with the words: *That was the last I ever saw of her.* Read his story quickly. Do you think it answers the question successfully?

The snow ¹*fell /* *was falling* thick on my windshield. My eyes were tired from all the whiteness. I wanted to stop, but I also wanted to get home. Then I ²*was seeing / saw* her standing by the side of the road.

She got in quickly. She ³*shivered / was shivering* from the cold. We soon started talking. She told me that she lived in the next town, and then she told me about how her husband ⁴*had been killing / had been killed* in a car crash on this very road, exactly one year ago.

Then suddenly she ⁵*was screaming / screamed* "Look out!" I looked and saw the car in front of me. I put on the brakes, the car skidded across the road and came to a stop. I ⁶*was shaking / shook* with fear. I turned to thank her because she

⁷*was saving / had saved* my life. However, when I looked around she ⁸*went / had gone*, and her door was open. I looked out and saw a dark figure ⁹*walk / walking* in the distance. It soon disappeared in the snow. That was the last I ever saw of her.

b Mark uses a variety of past tenses in his story. (Circle) the correct words.

WRITING TIP

Developing your ideas to write a story (1)

A Getting ideas is an extremely important part of writing a story. Let your imagination take control. Close your eyes and write down any ideas that come into your mind.

Ask yourself questions and write down your answers. Here are some examples for the story in Exercise 6a.

Who was she? *A girlfriend, a ghost, a mysterious stranger …*

Why was I with her? *She asked me for directions, I gave her a ride to the airport, I stopped to help her with a flat tire …*

Why didn't I see her again? *She went to live in another country, she disappeared, she died, she gave me her phone number but I lost it …*

B Use the combination you like best to create an outline for the story.

I was driving. I stopped to help a woman with a flat tire. We started talking. I didn't see the car in the middle of the road. She screamed to warn me. I didn't crash. I looked at her. Her door was open. I saw a figure walking along the road. It disappeared.

C Now ask yourself questions to develop the story. For example:
- What was the weather like?
- Where was I going?
- How was I feeling?
- Why did I stop?
- What did we talk about?

D Use the answers to these questions to develop your story. Remember:
- Use a good range of vocabulary (adjectives, adverbs, etc.) to make your story descriptive.
- Use a variety of past tenses.
- Link your sentences and paragraphs well.

c Write a story ending with the words: *And then the phone rang.*

1 Fill in the blanks

Complete the text with the words in the box.

between	have	wonder	might	message
neither	we are	~~can't~~	must	most

There _____can't_____ be many people who have never heard of the Bermuda Triangle. This area of

ocean [1] _____ Florida and Bermuda is one of the world's [2] _____ mysterious places.

Over a hundred ships and planes have been lost here. Many of these [3] _____ have been in

accidents or storms. But [4] _____ of these causes explains the mystery of Flight 19 – a U.S. Navy

training flight from Fort Lauderdale with the most modern technology. The radio operator back at base

[5] _____ have thought it was strange when he received a [6] _____ from the pilot saying they

were lost and that the sky seemed strange. His last communication was: "I don't know where

[7] _____ . It looks like we ...". They were never seen again. Many people [8] _____ why the

flight disappeared so suddenly. Some think it must [9] _____ been caught in a tropical storm. ☐ 9

2 Choose the correct answers

(Circle) the correct answer: a, b or c.

1 She _____ liked it. She left after 20 minutes.
   a must have   b might have   c (couldn't have)

2 We're coming to your city next week. Can you put us _____ for one or two nights, please?
   a up   b down   c in

3 Do you happen to know where _____?
   a they went   b did they go   c went they

4 I was in bed when the lights went _____ .
   a over   b about   c out

5 He might _____ called, but I wasn't home.
   a has   b had   c have

6 A window was broken at school today. I'm sure Zachary Gordon was tied _____ with it.
   a off   b up   c in

7 I wonder why _____ that.
   a she said   b said she   c did she say

8 I was looking for my keys, and I _____ across $10 behind the sofa.
   a found   b came   c went

9 There _____ have been 80,000 people at the game. It was so crowded.
   a couldn't   b must   c might   ☐ 8

3 Vocabulary

Change the underlined words. Use the correct form of the verbs in parentheses and a preposition.

1 My friend's uncle <u>died</u> last week. (pass) _passed away_
2 Suddenly, at midnight, all the lights in the house <u>stopped working</u>. (go) _____
3 I <u>met</u> my mother's best friend at the movies last night. (run) _____
4 Sorry I'm late. The train <u>stopped working</u>. (break) _____
5 The field was covered in water, so they <u>canceled</u> the game. (call) _____
6 Do you remember that I lost my backpack? Well, it <u>appeared</u> in the garage! (turn) _____
7 I was reading a magazine yesterday, and I <u>found</u> an interesting article. (come) _____
8 He invited me to a concert, but I <u>said no to</u> his invitation. (turn) _____
9 My brother and his girlfriend <u>ended their relationship</u> yesterday. (break) _____   ☐ 8

How did you do?

Total: ☐ 25

☺ Very good 25 – 20	☺ OK 19 – 16	☹ Review Unit 12 again 15 or less

13 Love

1 Grammar

★ Reported speech review

a Rewrite the sentences in direct speech.

1 The man told the woman that he was really scared of dogs.

"*I'm really scared of dogs* _____," the man told her.

2 Sue told her father that she would go to the grocery store with him on Saturday.

"_____," Sue told her father.

3 John explained he had to get up early in the morning to catch the train.

"_____," explained John.

4 Janet told us there had been an earthquake in China.

"_____," Janet told us.

5 Dad said he was sorry he couldn't get home earlier.

"_____," said Dad.

6 Ben told us he was going to Quito in the morning.

"_____," Ben told us.

7 Anna said she had to leave before eight o'clock.

"_____," said Anna.

8 Miguel said that he couldn't type very fast.

"_____," said Miguel.

b Rewrite the sentences. Use the words in parentheses.

1 "You must buy your girlfriend some flowers," Mom told me.

Mom __*told me that I had to buy*__ some flowers for my girlfriend.

2 "Tony is my brother, not my boyfriend," Anne said.

Anne _____ her brother, not her boyfriend.

3 "I did not steal the money," the man said.

The man _____ the money.

4 "I can't go on vacation in August," Tony explained.

Tony _____ on vacation in August.

5 "I have not learned anything for the test," Jane told us.

Jane _____ anything for the test.

6 "I'm going to marry Cathy," Nick told us.

Nick told us that _____ .

7 "I don't want to hear complaints all the time," the teacher said.

The teacher _____ hear complaints all the time.

8 "I'll give you the money back in three days," he promised me.

He _____ the money back in three days.

2 Grammar

✱ Reported questions

a Put the questions into reported speech.

1 "When is your birthday?" (The girl wanted to know ...)

   The girl wanted to know when my birthday was.

2 "Will we get to the concert on time?" (Jen asked ...)

   ....

3 "Can you install this game for me?" (Carol asked me ...)

   ....

4 "Why can't I stay up longer?" (My little sister asked ...)

   ....

5 "Where's the hospital?" (The driver wanted to know ...)

   ....

6 "Have you been to Canada?" (He asked me ...)

   ....

b Complete the conversation with the phrases in the box.

> don't think   was excellent   doesn't mean   I'll finish
> ~~Have you seen~~   Why's that   it was awful

Lucy: *Have you seen* Matrix Revolutions?

Liz: No, I haven't, and I ¹.......................... I want to.

Lucy: ².......................... ?

Liz: My friends have seen it, and they said
³.......................... .

Lucy: I find that surprising. I've only seen the first part, and
that ⁴.......................... .

Liz: I know, but that ⁵.......................... much!

Lucy: You're probably right, but I think ⁶..........................
watching it anyway.

c Complete the report on the conversation between Lucy and Liz.

Lucy asked Liz .....*whether*..... she had seen *Matrix
Revolutions*. Liz replied that she ¹.......................... , but
she ².......................... want to. Lucy ³..........................
to know why. Liz replied that her friends ⁴..........................
it, and they ⁵.......................... awful. Lucy answered that
she ⁶.......................... that surprising. She ⁷..........................
the first part, and that ⁸.......................... excellent. Liz
replied that she ⁹.......................... , but that
¹⁰.......................... much. Lucy replied that she
¹¹.......................... right, but she ¹²..........................
watching it anyway.

3 Vocabulary

✱ Appearance

Robert

Donna

Kevin

Jenny

a Write the names of the people.

1 Who is plump? .....*Kevin*.....

2 Who has a ponytail? ....

3 Who has a double chin?

   ....

4 Who has wrinkles on his
   forehead? ....

5 Who has a scar? ....

6 Who has freckles on her cheeks?

   ....

b Look at the pictures again and complete the sentences.

1 Robert has a .... on his
   head. He is rather short and he
   has .....*spiky*..... hair.

2 Jenny has .... hair.

3 Donna has her hair in a
   .... On her left arm, she
   has a .... of
   a dolphin.

4 Kevin has .... eyebrows.
   He has .... hair, a
   .... and .... on
   his forehead.

4 Vocabulary

✱ Personality

Complete the text. (Circle) **the correct answer: a, b, c or d.**

I have three sisters and two brothers. My oldest brother is Adam. Once I was sick for two weeks. Adam was really ¹ _considerate_ and took care of me. But sometimes Adam is really ² _____ . He likes to tell us what to do all the time and how we should do it. We often tell him to be more ³ _____ , but he doesn't listen. Eddie, my other brother, is the most ⁴ _____ of us all. He was always the best student in his class, and he finished college really quickly. The problem is that he never has any time for himself, but we tell him to be a little less ⁵ _____ and relax more. We all get along really well with my youngest sister Margaret, except when we try to interfere with her life. She is a very ⁶ _____ person, and she really doesn't like other people to tell her what to do!

1	a	(considerate)	b	ambitious	c	determined	d	imaginative
2	a	sensitive	b	independent	c	bossy	d	ambitious
3	a	imaginative	b	bossy	c	ambitious	d	considerate
4	a	bossy	b	ambitious	c	sensitive	d	insensitive
5	a	determined	b	imaginative	c	sensitive	d	considerate
6	a	independent	b	insensitive	c	considerate	d	sensitive

5 Grammar

✱ Reporting verbs

a (Circle) **the correct verbs.**

Tracey and Caroline were talking about going to the movies. Tracey ¹(said) / told that she ²wanted / wants to see a thriller. Caroline ³said / told that she ⁴will / would like to see a romantic movie. Tracey ⁵said / offered to go and get a newspaper. Caroline ⁶suggested / asked checking the movie listings on the Internet. She went online, but a few minutes later she ⁷said / told that there ⁸aren't / weren't any interesting movies playing. Tracey ⁹said / told Caroline that it ¹⁰might / will be better to rent a DVD and watch it at home. So Caroline ¹¹asked / said her to go and get a good DVD. Tracey ¹²said / told that she ¹³is / was happy to do that. Twenty minutes later she came back. She ¹⁴apologized / complained for choosing a thriller, but Caroline ¹⁵refused / invited to watch it!

b **Use the past tense form of the verbs in the box to write the sentences in reported speech.**

> explain ~~tell~~ refuse persuade beg suggest
> agree apologize

1 "Wash your hands before you sit down!" Mom said to my little brother.

   Mom told my little brother to wash his hands before
   he sat down.

2 "Please, please lend me your DVD player!" Pete said to me.

   _____

3 "I'm really sorry that I forgot about your birthday," Cathy said to her dad.

   _____

4 "All right. I'll make pizza for dinner," my mother said.

   _____

5 "I'm late because of the traffic," she said.

   _____

6 "I won't do it!" she said.

   _____

7 **Tom:** "I know you don't like basketball, but please will you watch the game with me, just this once?"

   Alan: "Oh, all right then. But just this once!"

   _____

8 "Let's play tennis," said Lucy.

   _____

6 Pronunciation

✱ Intonation in reported questions

a ▶ CD3 T35 Listen and repeat.

1 What's your favorite color?
2 How are you enjoying the meal?
3 When will you be back?
4 Do you often watch TV?

b ▶ CD3 T36 Listen and repeat.

1 He asked me what my favorite color was.
2 She asked them how they were enjoying the meal.
3 He asked her when she'd be back.
4 She asked me if I often watched TV.

7 Fiction in mind

a Read another extract from *Two Lives* by Helen Naylor. What is Huw's profession?

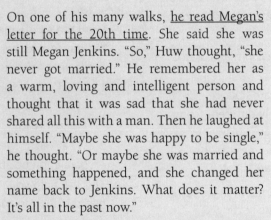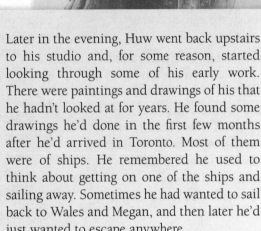

On one of his many walks, he read Megan's letter for the 20th time. She said she was still Megan Jenkins. "So," Huw thought, "she never got married." He remembered her as a warm, loving and intelligent person and thought that it was sad that she had never shared all this with a man. Then he laughed at himself. "Maybe she was happy to be single," he thought. "Or maybe she was married and something happened, and she changed her name back to Jenkins. What does it matter? It's all in the past now."

When he arrived back home that evening he told his family that he had made a decision: he was not going to write back to Megan. His life was here now. Better to let the past stay in the past.

Later in the evening, Huw went back upstairs to his studio and, for some reason, started looking through some of his early work. There were paintings and drawings of his that he hadn't looked at for years. He found some drawings he'd done in the first few months after he'd arrived in Toronto. Most of them were of ships. He remembered he used to think about getting on one of the ships and sailing away. Sometimes he had wanted to sail back to Wales and Megan, and then later he'd just wanted to escape anywhere.

He spent the next few hours lost in his thoughts. It was five o'clock in the morning when he looked at his watch and slowly went to bed, his head still full of the past.

(from Naylor H. *Two Lives*, CUP: p. 32)

b Read the extract again. All these statements are true. <u>Underline</u> the parts of the text that tell you the same thing.

1 Huw had read the letter before.
2 He had nice memories of Megan.
3 Huw decided something and then told other people.
4 Huw didn't want to think about things in the past.
5 Huw wasn't sure why he started to look at his early paintings.
6 Before, Huw had dreams of going to another place by ship.
7 Huw thought about these things for a long time.
8 When Huw went to bed, he was still thinking about his earlier life.

To find out if Huw goes back to Wales to find Megan, read the story!

8 Read

Read the article. For each question (circle) the correct answer.

Romeo and Juliet:
the greatest love story of all time

Since the invention of the motion picture in 1894, *Romeo and Juliet* has been one of the most popular stories in movies. Numerous movies have been based on Shakespeare's famous love story, the earliest dating back to 1900.

Many directors have taken this famous play and made it into a movie, trying to keep to the themes of the original story. One of them is Baz Luhrmann. His version of Romeo and Juliet, produced in 1996, has been described as an original, post-modern version of Shakespeare's tragic love story.

With this extremely successful movie, Luhrmann has managed to update the story by combining modern-day settings and characters with most of the original language. The story is set in Miami. The changes in the language, together with dramatic gun fights and passionate love scenes, make the story more accessible to modern audiences.

In Luhrmann's version of the movie, the main characters, Romeo (Leonardo DiCaprio) and Juliet (Clare Danes), are Miami teenagers in the nineties. Even though the setting of the movie is very unconventional, it contains all the themes of the original version because it does not change the story at all.

1 A lot of movies have been produced that are based on
   a William Shakespeare's play *Romeo and Juliet*.
   b a motion picture from 1894 called *Romeo and Juliet*.
   c an invention made by William Shakespeare in 1894.

2 Baz Luhrmann
   a is the only movie director who has tried to keep to the themes of the original play.
   b is one of the movie directors who have tried to keep to the themes of the original play.
   c produced his earliest version of *Romeo and Juliet* as early as 1900.

3 The language Luhrmann uses is
   a exactly the same as in Shakespeare's play.
   b completely different from Shakespeare's play.
   c almost the same as in Shakespeare's play.

4 Why did Luhrmann make some changes to the setting?
   a because he added gun fights and passionate love scenes
   b because he wanted to help people understand the story better
   c because teenagers in Miami speak a very strong dialect

5 Which of the following statements is true about Baz Luhrmann?
   a He produced a successful, but unconventional and provocative, version of the play.
   b He produced a modern, but not very successful, version of the play.
   c He produced a successful, but not very accessible, modern version of the play.

READING TIP

How to answer multiple-choice questions

In Unit 8 you saw how to do multiple-choice questions with listening. Here are some ideas for reading.

- Read the whole text first, but pause after each paragraph. Ask yourself:
  1 What's the main idea in the paragraph that I've just read?
  2 What might the next paragraph be about?
  This will help you to find the answers more easily later.

- Some of the answers use words or phrases from the text. Be careful. They might be the wrong answers! Look at the questions in Exercise 8. Which answers contain language from the text, but are clearly wrong?

- Sometimes answers are not directly in the text. Some questions ask for your ability to draw conclusions from what you are reading. Which questions in Exercise 8 can't be answered directly from the text?

Unit check

1 Fill in the blanks

Complete the text with the words in the box.

| ~~plump~~ short bad-tempered sensitive hair tattoo well-built ambitious determined ponytail |

My best friend is Carolyn. A year ago she started to exercise regularly, and now she's not ...._plump_......... anymore. She also changed her hairstyle. First, she had long ¹................ that she wore in a ²................ , but now her hair's ³................ . Carolyn's the best student in my class. She's really ⁴................ , and sometimes she is a little ⁵................ when she doesn't get top grades. But I like Carolyn a lot. When I have a problem, she's very ⁶................ . I want to learn from Carolyn. I'm going to exercise regularly, too. I'm very ⁷................ , and I won't give up until I am as ⁸................ as she is. But one thing's for sure: I'm not going to get a ⁹................ on my left arm. That's something I don't like so much about her!

| 9 |

2 Choose the correct answers

Circle the correct answer: a, b or c.

1 Jane said that she .... nervous.
   a (was) b were c be

2 She asked me if I .... seen her glasses.
   a have been b having c had

3 Your sister said that she .... to leave.
   a had b having c have

4 John promised that he .... study the words.
   a to b would c would to

5 They wanted to know when he .... back.
   a would come b will coming c would

6 I asked them if they .... help me.
   a be able to b able c could

7 They apologized for not .... on time.
   a being b to be c been

8 We asked them .... us an email.
   a writing b write c to write

9 I suggested .... Peter for some advice.
   a asking b to ask c ask

| 8 |

3 Vocabulary

In each line, underline the word that does not belong in the group.

	a	b	c	d
1	considerate	<u>long</u>	bossy	sensitive
2	bad-tempered	bossy	considerate	insensitive
3	wavy	long	straight	plump
4	bangs	tattoo	scar	freckles
5	beard	mustache	bushy eyebrows	well-built
6	broad-shouldered	spiky	plump	well-built
7	broad-shouldered	plump	straight	double chin
8	scar	freckles	wrinkles	eyebrows
9	ponytail	bangs	wavy	wrinkles

| 8 |

How did you do?

Total: | 25 |

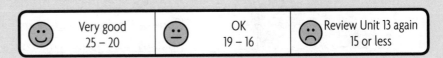

| ☺ | Very good 25 – 20 | ☺ | OK 19 – 16 | ☹ | Review Unit 13 again 15 or less |

14 Regret

1 Grammar

✱ Third conditional

a Match the sentences with the pictures A–D. Write 1–4 in the boxes.

1 If she'd studied harder for the test, she would have gotten a better grade.

2 If she hadn't studied hard for the test, she wouldn't have gotten such a good grade.

3 If we'd left earlier, we wouldn't have missed the train.

4 If we'd left any later, we would have missed the train.

b Complete the third conditional sentences with the correct form of the verbs.

1 I don't think so many people __*would have come*__ (come) to the concert if they __*'d known*__ (know) that the lead singer was sick.

2 What _____ you _____ (say) if I _____ (show) you the present earlier?

3 We _____ (save) a lot of money if we _____ (go) to a cheaper restaurant.

4 He _____ (not buy) such an expensive guitar if his father _____ (not give) him the money.

5 If she _____ (pass) her driving test, she _____ (drive) us to California.

6 Nobody _____ (hear) us if we _____ (not shout).

7 If you _____ (not run after) me, I _____ (not fall).

8 Why _____ he _____ (call) us if he _____ (not be) in trouble?

c Match the sentences below with the pictures A–G. Write 1–7 in the boxes. Then join the sentences using the third conditional.

1 One of Daniel's friends gave Daniel his ticket for a concert.

2 Daniel went to the concert.

3 He was standing next to a girl named Annie.

4 Annie and Daniel chatted.

5 The next evening, Daniel and Annie went out together.

6 They fell in love.

7 A year later they got married.

If one of Daniel's friends hadn't given Daniel his ticket, he wouldn't have gone to the concert. If Daniel hadn't gone to ....

2 Grammar

✱ *I wish / If only* for past situations

Write down a regret for each situation, starting your sentences with *I wish* or *If only*. Use an expression from the box for each sentence.

kick ball   drive so fast   break vase   play with pen   ~~slam door~~   buy sports car

1 *I wish I hadn't slammed the door.*

   The neighbors are really annoyed.

2 _____

   Where can I buy a new one now?

3 _____

   What will my parents say?

4 _____

   I'll never get rid of the stain on my jeans!

5 _____

   This is going to cost me money.

6 _____

   I have no money left.

3 Grammar

✱ *should / shouldn't have*

a Match the two parts of the sentences. Write a–f in the boxes.

1 I should listen to my parents `d`   a because I think they were right.
2 I should have listened to my parents ☐   b because it wasn't her fault.
3 I shouldn't have been angry with Lisa ☐   c before it is too late.
4 I shouldn't be angry with Lisa ☐   d because I think they are right.
5 I should write her an email ☐   e before it was too late.
6 I should have written her an email ☐   f because it isn't her fault.

b Write a response to these statements using *should've* or *shouldn't have* and a phrase from the box with the correct form of the verb.

~~leave earlier~~
call the police
take a sweater with her
take the risk
wear better shoes
buy something earlier

1 I missed the bus. *You should've left earlier.*
2 She's feeling cold. _____
3 He lost all his money. _____
4 They can't find a present for their mom. _____
5 They saw that the man had a gun. _____
6 He slipped on the sidewalk and broke his leg. _____

4 Pronunciation

★ should / shouldn't have

a ▶ CD3 T37 **Listen and repeat.**

1 You (shouldn't have) done that.
2 I shouldn't have listened to her.
3 Oh, no, you shouldn't have.
4 We should have bought it.
5 They didn't tell us, but they should have.
6 You should have written to me.

b ▶ CD3 T37 **Listen again.** Underline *should/shouldn't have* when it is pronounced fully. (Circle) it when it is pronounced quickly and sounds like "shouldenev" or "shouldev."

5 Vocabulary

★ Anger

a **Complete the text.** (Circle) the correct word: a, b, c or d.

A few weeks ago, I wanted to go on a bike tour with three friends. The evening before the tour, Jeremy and Laura called to say they couldn't come. I was ¹ _furious_ . I was especially ² _____ with Jeremy because he was the one who had initially suggested going on the bike tour. Anyway, the next morning I was sorry for losing my ³ _____ and called Jeremy to apologize. But he didn't even want to talk. He was so ⁴ _____ ! I ⁵ _____ my cool and said, "OK. If you're so ⁶ _____ and lose your temper so easily, it's your problem and not mine!" You know what? He started having ⁷ _____ and bit ⁸ _____ for shouting at him! I don't know what he meant! But what could I do? I think I can only ⁹ _____ and wait for him to cool down again!

1 a (furious)   b hot-headed   c mad at   d calm
2 a hot-headed   b temper   c upset   d mad
3 a head   b tantrum   c calm   d temper
4 a cool   b hot-headed   c upset   d calm
5 a got   b had   c kept   d bit
6 a indignant   b calm   c cool   d hot-headed
7 a a temper   b a tantrum   c my head off   d his cool
8 a my head off   b a tantrum   c his cool   d his temper
9 a be calm   b have a tantrum   c be upset   d bite his head off

b (Vocabulary bank) **Read the dialogue and** (circle) **the correct words.**

Will: Hey, Joe? What's up? You look pretty ¹(upset) / bitter.

Joe: Nothing really. I just had a ²hot / heated argument with Rachel.

Will: Not again. What was it about this time?

Joe: Music. She basically told me that all the music I like is awful.

Will: That's pretty rude.

Joe: At first, I think she was joking. But after a while I got a little ³mad / irritated. So I tried to change the subject. But she wouldn't stop. So I told her that she didn't know anything about music! Then she looked at me the ⁴right / wrong way and acted all ⁵indignant / bitter as if I'd said something really unfair. She wanted ME to say sorry to her.

Will: So what did you do?

Joe: Well, I acted ⁶irritated / outraged. I wanted her to feel that she had made me really angry.

Will: Did it work?

Joe: Not really. She just walked off in a really ⁷bad / angry mood.

Will: So what are you going to do?

Joe: Nothing. I'll wait a while. Then next time I see her, she'll pretend to be ⁸bitter / indignant and let me know that she hasn't forgotten. And then we'll find something new to argue about. Same as always.

Will: Well, I suppose that's what sisters are for.

Joe: Exactly.

6 Study help

✱ How to complete cloze texts

Sometimes you have to fill in the blanks in a text with one word and no clues are given.

- It's important that you read the whole text first. Don't focus on the blanks, but try to understand what the general meaning of the text is. Look at the title, too!

- Carefully study the words before and after the blank. Try to find clues that help you to identify the meaning of the word needed. Is it the opposite of something? Is it an example of something? Is it a synonym? Is it part of an expression?

- Try to identify the type of word that's needed. For example, is it an article? A preposition? A noun? Look at number 1 in the text. The words before the blank are: *can be caused*. This tells us that the sentence is a simple present passive construction. The words after the blank tell us what the cause is, so what is the missing word?

- If the word you need to fill in is a verb, make sure it agrees with the subject that it goes with. Don't forget the third person -*s*!

- If you are not sure about a word, try to guess the answer and write it down on a piece of paper. Then come back later to the blanks you found difficult to do. You will sometimes find it easier to find the right word the second time around.

- Read the whole text again and check that the words you have filled in make sense.

Complete the text with one word for each blank.

What is anger?
And what can you do about it?

According to psychologists, anger ____*is*____ a feeling. As with other emotional states, we notice changes when we are angry. There are biological changes, for example. Our heart rate and blood pressure go up, as do the levels of our energy hormones.

Anger can be caused [1]_____ both external and internal events. You could be angry at a specific [2]_____ , such as a classmate or a teacher, or an event could make you angry. For example, maybe you have [3]_____ your bus, or it starts raining and you [4]_____ planned to go for a walk. Or your anger could be caused by worrying [5]_____ your personal problems. Memories of very negative events can also trigger angry feelings.

However, you can control your angry feelings with simple techniques. There are books and courses [6]_____ can teach you relaxation techniques, and once you have learned the techniques, you can use them in different situations. If you are in a relationship where both of you are quick-tempered, it might be a good idea for both of you [7]_____ learn the techniques. Practice the techniques daily and learn to use [8]_____ when you're in a difficult situation.

Skills in mind

7 Write a story (2)

a John's teacher asked him to write a story with the title: "An Embarrassing Situation." Read his answer. Why was the situation embarrassing?

WRITING TIP

Developing your ideas to write a story (2)

In Unit 12, you were given the last line of a story and asked to complete it. Here, you are given the title.

- Don't start writing without having a clear plan of what you are going to write.

- Develop the storyline first. Have you ever been on a dangerous journey? Has someone you know told you about a dangerous journey?

- If you don't have a story, try to invent one. First of all, write the storyline. How does it begin? How does it develop? How does it end?

- Include interesting details, but not too many!

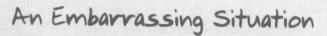

An Embarrassing Situation

I was on vacation with two of my friends, and we were staying in a hotel. The soccer World Cup was starting, and we all wanted to watch it. We decided to watch it in my room because there was a TV there, but we just couldn't get a picture. We kept pressing the channel button, but we couldn't get it to work.

Finally, we decided to call someone in reception and ask them to look at it. When the man arrived, he looked at the remote and calmly pressed the "on" button. Then he gave it back to me, and I pressed the button for the right channel!

b The writer gives the events, but the text does not contain much detail, so it isn't very interesting. Read the question prompts. Think of answers to them and write them down.

1 Where was the vacation? When? What was the place like? What was the hotel like?

2 How did you feel when you noticed that the TV didn't work? Why?

3 How long did you wait before you called reception? Had the game already started?

4 How did you feel when you realized you hadn't noticed the TV was not turned on? Did you later tell your friends about what had happened? Why? / Why not?

c Rewrite the text using the ideas you wrote in Exercise 7b to make it more interesting.

d Write a story with the title "A Dangerous Journey."

Unit check

1 Fill in the blanks

Complete the text with the words in the box.

furious ~~letter~~ keep regretting hot-headed difficult temper work tantrum mad

Dear Maria,

Thanks you for your ___letter___ . I'm afraid it's really not very easy to advise you. You had a fight with your boyfriend and lost your ¹_____ , and now you are ²_____ it. You say in your letter that your boyfriend is quite a ³_____ person, but it seems that it is ⁴_____ for you to ⁵_____ your cool, too. Now you are ⁶_____ with him, but maybe you should understand that he is also ⁷_____ at you. Perhaps you could learn to relax a little more and avoid having a ⁸_____ when you are arguing with someone you like. Maybe you can ⁹_____ something out together.

Yours, Barbara

☐ 9

2 Choose the correct answers

Circle the correct answer: a, b or c.

1 If I _____ sick, I would have gone to school.
   a (hadn't been) b were not c am not

2 They would not _____ in love if they hadn't met.
   a fall b had fallen c have fallen

3 If the police hadn't come, the man would have _____ .
   a escaping b escaped c escape

4 That's going to hit you! Look _____ !
   a in b out c under

5 I'm so curious. I wish I _____ her before.
   a asked b been asked c had asked

6 I missed the bus. I _____ left so late.
   a hadn't b should have c shouldn't have

7 We should have left before they _____ .
   a arrived b would arrive c arrive

8 This is so complicated, I don't think we can _____ it out.
   a sort b stop c avoid

9 I am so full! If only I _____ so much.
   a not eaten b wouldn't have eaten
   c hadn't eaten

☐ 8

3 Vocabulary

Replace the underlined words so that the sentences make sense.

1 I don't know what I said to Jo, but she bit my arm off. ___head___

2 In an emergency, you should try to keep your calm. _____

3 My dad is really heat-headed.

   _____

4 Mr. Riley lost his mood today.

   _____

5 Ben is in a tantrum mood today.

   _____

6 I forgot Valentine's Day and my girlfriend is temper. _____

7 Amy always looks at me the wrong time. I wonder if she dislikes me.

   _____

8 They started a(n) irritated argument because of soccer. _____

9 When Mom told Tim he couldn't have ice cream, Tim had a temper.

   _____

☐ 8

How did you do?

Total: ☐ 25

| 😊 | Very good 25 – 20 | 😐 | OK 19 – 16 | 😟 | Review Unit 14 again 15 or less |

15 Hopes and fears

1 Grammar

✱ Non-defining relative clauses

a Complete the sentences with the correct relative clause in the box.

where her family has a restaurant	which I have read five times
which is not far from San Francisco	which was why I couldn't go to school
who is still very popular	which I know I wrote down
~~where you can find beautiful beaches~~	whose name I've forgotten

1 I love going on vacation to Brazil, *where you can find beautiful beaches* .

2 Madonna, _____ , had her first hit in the 1980s.

3 Karen's best friend, _____ , is from China.

4 She lives in Seoul, _____ .

5 I had a nasty cold, _____ .

6 *The Hobbit*, _____ , is my favorite book.

7 He is Californian and was born in Santa Cruz, _____ .

8 I've lost your address, _____ .

b Complete the text with *who, whose, which* or *where*.

Mark O'Brian, _who_ was on his way to work early last Tuesday morning, was driving down North Lane when he was shocked by something he saw.

A driver, [1]_____ must have driven down the same street only a few minutes before, had lost control of his car. The car, [2]_____ had landed on its roof, burst into flames immediately.

Mr. O'Brian, [3]_____ quick thinking helped save the driver's life, got out of his car and saw that there was a man in the driver's seat. Mark called the fire department and then ran back to his own car, [4]_____ he kept a fire extinguisher. He rushed back to the scene just as another man was approaching.

O'Brian and the other man, [5]_____ has not been seen since the accident, managed to put out the fire.

They then broke the passenger window with a rock and freed the driver, [6]_____ luckily was not seriously injured. He was taken to the hospital, [7]_____ his condition has been described as comfortable.

c Join the sentences using *who, which, where* or *whose*. Sometimes you will need to change the order of the clauses. You will not need the underlined words.

1 Joanne speaks six languages. <u>She</u> lives next door.

Joanne, who lives next door, speaks six languages.

2 I love scuba diving in the Indian Ocean. You can still find a lot of attractive fish <u>there</u>.

_____

3 Next month, Stephanie will move to Boston. Her sister has an apartment <u>there</u>.

_____

4 Alex is getting married next year. <u>His</u> sister studies with me.

_____

5 Carolina has won the lottery. <u>She</u> lives next door to me.

_____

6 My new computer is fantastic. I got <u>it</u> for a very good price.

_____

2 Grammar and pronunciation

✱ Defining vs. non-defining relative clauses

a Check (✔) if the sentence is correct. If the sentence is wrong, write an *X* and insert or remove the commas.

1 Flying which so many people are afraid of is actually the safest way to travel. **✗**

   Flying, which so many people are afraid of,
   is actually the safest way to travel.

2 She's the girl that I told you about. ☐

3 He's the actor, that's afraid of clowns. ☐

4 Where's the huge spider that was in the bathroom earlier? ☐

5 I have to deliver this newspaper to number 13 where that big dog lives. ☐

6 Isn't she the actress, who's afraid of butterflies? ☐

7 My dad is allergic to cats which are my favorite animals. ☐

8 That's the man whose dog bit my brother. ☐

b ▶ **CD3 T38** Listen to the sentences in Exercise 2a and check your answers. Where can you hear the pauses?

c ▶ **CD3 T38** Listen again and repeat the sentences.

3 Vocabulary

✱ Adjectives with prefixes

a Complete the text with the correct form of the adjectives in parentheses. One of the adjectives stays the same.

Here are two things I hope will change in the future. The first one is about some of the people that I work with at the tourist information office. They're so _unhelpful_ (helpful)! It's embarrassing sometimes how ¹............... (polite) they can be to visitors from other countries. Even my boss gets ²............... (patient) sometimes when people can't speak English well. It makes me feel really ³............... (comfortable).

Secondly, I want all the ⁴............... (responsible) people in the world to stop destroying our planet. Too many politicians seem to be ⁵............... (concerned) about pollution and cutting down trees. I wish countries would make it ⁶............... (legal) to do things like this. It's so ⁷............... (healthy) for our planet. I suppose this is just an ⁸............... (possible) dream, though, and I'm ⁹............... (afraid) it will never happen.

Vocabulary bank Complete the dialogues with the opposite forms of the adjectives in the box. There are two words you won't need.

> sincere   rational   able   ~~personal~~   attractive   complete   probable   literate   mature   accurate

1	A: She's not a very warm human being, is she?	B: No, she's very ___impersonal___ .
2	A: Does she ever mean what she says?	B: No, she's really _____ .
3	A: He's a great actor, but he's not good-looking.	B: He is very _____ .
4	A: Did Beethoven finish his tenth symphony?	B: No, it was _____ .
5	A: Her fear of gloves just doesn't make sense.	B: Yes, it's really _____ .
6	A: Do you think Malta will ever win the World Cup?	B: It's highly _____ .
7	A: Did you hear those stupid jokes he told?	B: I know. He's so _____ .
8	A: Can he read or write?	B: No, he's _____ .

4 Grammar

✳ Definite, indefinite and no article

a Complete the sentences with *the, a* or nothing.

1 I take ___a___ shower at least once a day.

2 This is _____ new school that I told you about.

3 His brother works as _____ pilot for American Airlines.

4 Lydia plays _____ drums in a band.

5 If he doesn't feel better tomorrow, we'll have to take him to _____ hospital.

6 Can you pass me _____ sugar, please?

7 When does _____ game start?

8 I'm allergic to _____ school!

b Check (✔) if the line is correct. If the line has an article (*a, an,* or *the*) that should not be there, write the word in the blank.

Yesterday my friend Linda and I had lunch at the pizzeria	1 ___✔___
behind our school. I know Linda isn't crazy about ~~the~~ pizza,	2 ___the___
but I think she came along because of me. At the table next to us,	3 _____
there were two guys from our class. The one of them was really funny.	4 _____
He tried to imitate all the people in the pizzeria. We couldn't stop	5 _____
laughing. But there were some the customers who did not like	6 _____
the fact that two boys were imitating them. They complained to	7 _____
the owner of the restaurant, and he came over and told them to stop.	8 _____
It was too bad because Linda and I were really having a fun!	9 _____

5 Vocabulary

✳ Phrasal verbs with *through*

Complete the sentences with the correct form of phrasal verbs with *through*.

1 Good news! I managed to ___get through___ 80 pages of my reading assignment last night.

2 I just can't _____ another of Uncle Ted's vacation videos! They're so boring!

3 I _____ my driving test. I didn't make a single mistake!

4 I need to _____ my notes tonight. I have an important test tomorrow.

5 OK, I'll _____ it all one more time. Starting from the beginning, ...

Culture in mind

a ▶ CD3 T39 Listen to part of an article about arithmophobia. Answer the questions.

1   What is arithmophobia?
2   What is triskaidekaphobia?
3   What will Stephen King <u>not</u> do when he gets to page 49 of a book?
4   What does Michael Ballack wear for games?

b Read the rest of the article about arithmophobia. Then write the name of the phobias in the chart.

1. The fear of the number 4	
2. The fear of the number 8	
3. The fear of the number 5	

ARITHMOPHOBIA

People aren't only afraid of the number 13. In China, Japan and Korea, the number four is <u>regarded as</u> an unlucky number. The word for the number four sounds similar to the word for *death*. <u>Consequently</u>, many buildings either do not have a fourth floor, or elevators label the floor with the first letter of the word instead of the number four. This <u>irrational</u> fear is called tetraphobia.

The fear of the number eight is called octophobia. Some people who fear the

number eight aren't just afraid of the number. They are also afraid of the "figure eight" – the shape the eight makes. For example, they may feel frightened if they see a symbol that has a similar shape.

Many people think some numbers are unlucky, but it doesn't affect their lives that much. They may stop reading a page of a book with a certain number, or they might not stay in a hotel with a certain room number. But for some people, arithmophobia can be a real problem. They may feel <u>anxious</u> and stressed when they see a certain number. Others may be afraid of all numbers. This can make math and daily life very difficult.

Scientist aren't sure what causes arithmophobia. Some think a person might have had a bad experience <u>related to</u> a certain number. For example, a family member might have died on a certain date, like August 5. A person may then develop quintaphobia and have bad feelings and fears about the number 5.

c Match the words below to the <u>underlined</u> words in the article.

1   extreme uneasiness or fear about something   *anxious*

2   so   ....

3   thought to be   ....

4   connected with   ....

5   not based on reason or clear thinking   ....

7 Listen

▶ CD3 T40 Listen to an interview with a psychologist about why people like frightening stories and the effect such stories can have on people. What does the psychologist say? Take notes to complete the sentences.

1 People like telling frightening stories so they can _entertain others_ .

2 Most of the stories have a
-- .

3 If a story has comic relief, we
-- .

4 Healthy adult people are not harmed by listening to frightening stories because
-- .

5 Fairy tales are important for children because
-- .

6 A child who listens to fairy tales also
-- .

7 Some horror movies are
-- .

LISTENING TIP

Note taking

- Before you listen, first read the task carefully. It gives you important information about what to expect in the listening. Then read the questions. You may want to <u>underline</u> key words in the questions. Look at the instructions for Exercise 7. What are the key words?

- Try to predict what kinds of answers you are expected to give. Does the question ask for some specific information (for example, a person's age or physical appearance)? What kind of language might you need to answer the question?

- Listen carefully to the information given.

- Write clear answers that are not too long, but have all the necessary information. Use numerals and abbreviations (*16* instead of *sixteen*, *km* instead of *kilometers*).

- Stay calm if you can't answer each question immediately. If you can't answer a question, leave it out. Try to complete the missing answers during the second listening.

Unit check

1 Fill in the blanks

Complete the text with the words in the box.

> unafraid   unconcerned   through   that   who
> where   since   people   across   ~~looking~~

I was ___looking___ through some old photos recently when I came ¹_____ one of Trevor,
²_____ was my favorite cousin. It reminded me of the summer I spent with him when I was eight.
He lived on a street ³_____ had a lot of old, empty houses. At night, it was scary walking past
those houses, ⁴_____ I thought I could hear noises and see faces in the windows. I imagined
⁵_____ going ⁶_____ the walls. One night, I awoke to see Trevor sitting on the window ledge
with his legs outside, talking. I called his name, but he was asleep. My aunt came in and took him back
to bed. She seemed ⁷_____ about how close her son was to falling from the second floor. "Oh, he's
always sleepwalked. He'll be fine." She was so calm and reassuring that I've been ⁸_____ of
that neighborhood ever ⁹_____ .

☐ 9

2 Choose the correct answers

Circle the correct answer: a, b or c.

1   I love Italy, _____ you can get such great
    ice cream!
    a (where)   b who   c which

2   My sister works as _____ in Mexico City.
    a lawyer   b a lawyer   c the lawyer

3   Brasilia, _____ is the capital of Brazil, is a great city.
    a where   b who   c which

4   This is the person _____ car was stolen.
    a that   b who   c whose

5   What's the name of the TV show _____ you saw?
    a that   b where   c who

6   Michael Jackson, _____ lived at Neverland
    Ranch, was a pop legend.
    a where   b who   c which

7   My parents always go to _____ early in the
    morning.
    a the work   b a work   c work

8   Genghis Khan, the great warrior, was afraid
    of _____ .
    a cats   b a cat   c the cats

9   It was difficult to _____ through such a
    boring movie.
    a sit   b go   c sail

☐ 8

3 Vocabulary

Complete the sentences with a word beginning with a prefix.

1   It's really ___irresponsible___ to leave a dog in a hot car. Shame on you!
2   Isn't it _____ to go through a red light? Why didn't you stop?
3   There are some really _____ computers in the TechWorld sale – under $500.
4   They want people to wear _____ clothing to their wedding. Strange, isn't it?
5   Pizza, burgers and french fries sounds like a very _____ diet to me.
6   It's very _____ to cough without covering your mouth.
7   I'm so tired! My new bed is so _____ that I couldn't get any sleep.
8   He's totally _____ about his test. He thinks he'll sail through it.
9   She's _____ to talk to you right now. She'll call you back.

☐ 8

How did you do?

Total: ☐ 25

| | Very good 25 – 20 | | OK 19 – 16 | | Review Unit 15 again 15 or less |

16 Happiness

1 Grammar

✳ be used to

a Match the two parts of the sentences. Then match the sentences with the pictures. Write 1–6 in the boxes.

1 I'm not used to getting up early,

2 We have to wear a uniform in our new school,

3 All the stores close at lunchtime here,

4 My little sister was sick on our trip

5 My dad doesn't like his new office

6 Can I have a knife and fork please?

a and I don't like it because I'm used to wearing what I like.

b so I'm still really tired in the mornings.

c I'm not used to eating with chopsticks.

d because she's not used to traveling in the car.

e but I'm used to everything staying open all the time.

f because he's used to working from home.

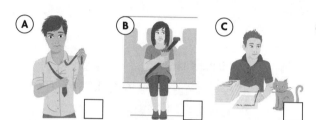

b Complete the sentences. Use the correct form of *used to* and the verbs in the box.

~~drive~~   eat   laugh   play   speak   wear

1 My father _used to drive_ a big, old, black Ford.

2 I _____ at his jokes, but now I think he's just immature.

3 My mother _____ Spanish, but she's forgotten almost all of it now.

4 _____ you _____ shorts when you were a little boy?

5 My sister and I _____ video games together, but now she's away at college.

6 I _____ (not) fast food, but now I eat it all the time!

c Complete the sentences with the correct form of the verbs in parentheses.

1 When I was younger, I used to __speak__ (speak) French, but I've forgotten it all.

2 I'm used to _____ (get) lots of emails every day.

3 A: This coffee is very strong.

   B: No problem. I'm used to _____ (drink) strong coffee.

4 They didn't use to _____ (care) about what other people think of them.

5 He used to _____ (live) in a houseboat on the Seine River, but he had to sell the boat.

6 She used to _____ (run) for an hour every day, but she can't anymore because of a problem with her knee.

7 Are you used to _____ (live) in the U.S. now, or do you still find it strange?

8 When he was young, he used to _____ (be) poor, but now he's rich, and he's used to _____ (buy) anything he wants!

2 Vocabulary

✱ Expressions with *feel*

a Paul wrote about his feelings in his computer diary. Read his diary entry and complete it.
Circle the correct word: a, b, c or d.

About five years ago, my favorite song was "And I Love Her" by the Beatles. It feels
¹ ___*strange*___ to say that now that I <u>do</u> love someone. I sometimes feel kind of weird.
For example, I feel a little ² _____ because I know that many other people are
feeling ³ _____ while I'm in love. I really feel ⁴ _____ them. When I walk
along the streets with my girlfriend, I also feel a little ⁵ _____ . It seems like
the whole world is looking at us! A week ago I felt ⁶ _____ to talk to my older
brother about my problems. He says I should just feel ⁷ _____ that I will grow
up. What does that mean? I am grown up. I'm just not feeling ⁸ _____ walking
around holding hands with someone with other people staring at us! Oh, no! I'm
feeling ⁹ _____ . I'm so glad nobody can read this.

	a		b		c		d	
1	a	up to	b	strange	c	cold	d	scared
2	a	up to	b	fine	c	guilty	d	comfortable
3	a	lonely	b	confident	c	fine	d	stupid
4	a	sorry for	b	up to	c	the need	d	confident
5	a	cold	b	up to	c	uncomfortable	d	fine
6	a	the need	b	cold	c	weird	d	lonely
7	a	the need	b	sorry for	c	confident	d	up to
8	a	comfortable	b	fine	c	up to	d	the need
9	a	the need	b	fine	c	cold	d	stupid

3 Grammar

✳ Phrasal verbs

a Complete the sentences with the correct form of one of the phrasal verbs in parentheses.

1 We have a problem, but I'm sure we can ___work___ it ___out___ . (work out / pick up)

2 I _____ Nick the other day when I was on First Avenue. (give up / bump into)

3 They didn't talk to each other for a year, but they have _____ their problems _____ now. (sort out / take after)

4 He really _____ his mother's side of the family. (give up / take after)

5 We really can't _____ his behavior any more! (put up / put up with)

6 We have to tell them the truth. We can't just _____ something _____ . (make up / give up)

7 This car is really old. I hope it's not going to _____ . (give up / break down)

8 Our friends _____ us _____ when we were in Miami. (put up / make up)

b Put the words in the correct order to make sentences.

1 you / to / up / doesn't / look / he   *He doesn't look up to you.* _____

2 ran / he / from / away / her   _____

3 each / well / other / we / along / get / with   _____

4 our / forward / look / we / to / vacations   _____

5 put / for / night / a / can / we / up / him / with   _____

4 Pronunciation

✳ Stress in phrasal verbs

a ▶ CD3 T41   Listen and ⟨circle⟩ the prepositions that are weak. Underline the prepositions that are stressed.

1 a I think we can work it <u>out</u>.
   b He didn't say a word and ran ⟨out⟩ of the house.

2 a Pick your coat up.
   b She picked up her pen.

3 a I've given up sugar.
   b I've given them up.

4 a The plane took off.
   b He took off his shoes.

b ▶ CD3 T41   Listen again, check and repeat.

5 Vocabulary

Vocabulary bank   Complete the sentences with the words in the box.

| a thing | the weather | at home | free |
| out of place | awful | feel | way |

1 I'm just going to give you a small injection. You won't feel ___a thing___ .

2 The lights went out, so we had to feel our _____ to the emergency exit.

3 I feel _____ about what I said to Danny about his girlfriend, but someone had to tell him.

4 I felt really _____ at the party, so I left early.

5 I love visiting my Aunt Abby. She really makes me feel _____ .

6 I'm learning how to dance the tango, and I'm just about getting the _____ of it.

7 Feel _____ to turn on the TV or use the computer while we're gone.

8 I don't think I'm going out tonight. I feel a little under _____ .

6 Fiction in mind

a You are going to read an extract from *A Matter of Chance*. Paul Morris's happy life in Italy changes when his wife dies suddenly. Years later, he reflects on how he feels about his wife's tragic accident.

While you read the extract, complete the text with the words in the box.

been   alone   across   ~~had~~   to talk   all   that   life

Jacky. What can I tell you about Jacky?

I can tell you how she looked that bright February morning when she stepped out into the new sun, as the snow was falling off all the roofs, as she went out to buy something for a dress she was making. For a special dinner – we ____had____ been married for three years.

I have a movie library of her in the back of my head: in the office; our first Christmas together, skiing in Scotland; the wedding; the trip ¹_____ France to our new home in Italy; and ... and ... I also have 10 photographs of her that I took. Just 10 out of the hundreds.

Afterward, when I was able to, I looked through all the photos of our ²_____ together and carefully chose the 10 I liked best. I then had them enlarged, and put them in a special photo album. Which I have never opened since. ³_____ this was many years ago. I am an old man now.

An old man full of memories, and full of thoughts about what could have ⁴_____ .

An old man who often thinks about the way that one tiny chance happening can change someone's life: the roof-tile falls a second earlier or a second later, she goes toward a different store, she goes toward the same store a different way, she meets a friend and stops ⁵_____ , she doesn't meet a friend and stop to talk, the traffic lights change as she gets to the crossing ... or ...

Such a tiny little chance ⁶_____ she was there then and the roof-tile was there then. Such a tiny little chance that left me, at 27 years of age, ⁷_____ in a foreign country. Italy. So much hope. Such a bright future. Such an exciting thing to do. An adventure. To go and to start a new life in Italy.

(from Hill, D.A. [1999] *A Matter of Chance*, CUP: pp. 7–9)

b Read the extract again and answer the questions.

1 What was the name of the narrator's wife? _____

2 Where was the narrator's wife killed? _____

3 How old was the narrator when his wife was killed? _____

4 Where did the tragic event happen? _____

7 Everyday English

Underline the correct options.

1 A: I'm thirsty.
   B: Same *here* / *me*! Let's get a drink.

2 A: Do you like Thomas Groves?
   B: Yes, I do! *Between* / *For* you and me, I'm hoping he'll ask me to go out one day.

3 I didn't want to apologize at first, but *on* / *in* the end, I thought it was the best thing to do.

4 No, I don't hate soccer. I just think there are better sports, *it's* / *that's* all.

5 A: San Francisco is the most beautiful city in the world.
   B: In *more* / *other* words, you think it's more beautiful than Rome or Paris? You're crazy!

6 A: Let's go into town.
   B: No, I'm really busy. Then *as well* / *again*, a break might be good for me. OK, let's go!

Skills in mind

8 Write

a Read Joanne's essay about family life. Complete her text with the correct statements (a–f). There is one statement you won't need.

  a   However, it is also true that things are not always easy.
  b   In conclusion, how would I respond if I were asked if I wanted to leave home?
  c   Personally, I would not want to be on my own too soon.
  d   I would love to be totally independent.
  e   Many of my friends would love to be independent from their parents as soon as possible.
  f   It's great to be part of a happy family.

"Happiness is having a large, loving, caring family in another city."
Discuss this statement and give your own opinion.

1 _____ It is fun to be with people who like you. It is good to feel the warmth and the love of the ones who care for you. It is fantastic when you can turn to them when you have problems.

2 _____ Young people want to develop their own personality. Parents often think they know better. They find it difficult to accept that their sons or their daughters want to live and think differently from how they used to live and think when they were young themselves. Consequently, young people are often frustrated and believe their parents do not understand them.

3 _____ They would love to have their own place where they can live the life they imagine must be ideal. They think that not having a

parent who tells them to clean their room or get up at a certain time must be paradise.

4 _____ First of all, there is the financial situation. Having your own place costs a lot of money. Secondly, being completely on your own also means a lot of responsibility. For example, I admit I like to be reminded occasionally of urgent things I have forgotten to do (although I would never admit that to my parents!). And thirdly, if members of a family accept that everybody is an individual and needs a certain amount of freedom, life with a family can be really fun.

5 _____ I would say that I am happy living with my family for now, and I'll wait to move out.

---

b Write an essay of about 300 words to discuss the following statement and give your own opinion: *The only way to happiness is by helping others.*

WRITING TIP

Developing a discursive essay (2)

● In order to make your points clearly and effectively, develop a clear progression of your argument.

● Decide how to introduce the topic, how to organize your ideas into paragraphs and how to conclude.

● Build each of your paragraphs around one particular point or idea. One effective way of doing this is to start each individual paragraph with a general statement (often called a topic sentence) to introduce the main idea of the paragraph. Add further sentences to support the idea.

Unit check

1 Fill in the blanks

Complete the text with the words in the box.

| told   used to   takes after   strange   ~~put me up~~ |
| puts up with   feel   look up to   sorry   felt |

My cousin Anna ...*put me up*... for a night when I visited Chicago. Anna has five brothers and sisters, and her house is complete chaos. I'm ¹ _____ living with just my parents, so it felt ² _____ at first. I feel kind of ³ _____ for her. I really don't know how she ⁴ _____ all the noise! Her two younger sisters really ⁵ _____ her. They even copy the way she dresses and talks! Anna ⁶ _____ her mom, and when I mentioned this, Anna ⁷ _____ me that everyone says this, so I ⁸ _____ a little stupid. It wasn't very relaxing, but I enjoyed staying there, as they made me ⁹ _____ at home.

[ ] 9

2 Choose the correct answers

(Circle) the correct answer: a, b or c.

1 When I was younger, I _____ speak Spanish.
   a (used to)   b was used to   c 'm used to

2 I'm used to _____ late.
   a stay up   b staying up   c stayed

3 I can't believe it. The car's broken _____ again.
   a up   b out   c down

4 He _____ into her at a party last night.
   a crashed   b bumped   c danced

5 I don't mind helping him. I'm used to _____ for others.
   a care   b caring   c caring about

6 I _____ to eat vegetables, but now I eat a lot of them.
   a didn't use   b didn't used   c used

7 He is cold because he is not used to _____ in a country like this.
   a live   b living   c lives

8 I shouldn't have done it. I'm really feeling _____!
   a up to   b fine   c guilty

9 After a year of living in Greece, he'd _____ up the language.
   a picked   b talked   c taken

[ ] 8

3 Vocabulary

Underline the correct words.

1 I'm feeling really *strange / confident / lonely* about my driving test. I know I'm going to pass.

2 She's feeling a little *beneath / below / under* the weather today. She's going to stay in bed.

3 Don't feel sorry *for / about / with* him. It's his own fault.

4 The dentist took out a tooth, but I didn't feel a *pain / hurt / thing*.

5 It's hot, and I'm on vacation. I feel the *want / need / wish* for ice cream!

6 It's normal to feel out of *room / place / face* on your first day at a new school.

7 I'd love to go on a long walk with you, but I don't really feel *on / up / out* to it today.

8 Please feel *free / open / up* to take anything you want from the fridge.

9 I felt really *stupid / confident / strange* when I gave the teacher the wrong answer.

[ ] 8

How did you do?

Total: [ ] 25

 Very good 25 – 20   OK 19 – 16   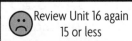 Review Unit 16 again 15 or less

Vocabulary bank

Unit 3 Collocations with *talk* and *speak*

talk

1 **make small talk** = social conversation about unimportant things
We **made small talk** before the meeting because we didn't know each other well.

2 **to talk back** = to reply in a rude way to someone you should be polite to
Our teacher was really angry with Alex because he **talked back** to her.

3 **to talk + noun** = to talk about a particular subject
When Mary and Jane get together, they just **talk clothes** all the time.

4 **to talk shop** = to talk about your job with the people you work with, even when you are not at work
My mom and dad work in the same bank, and in the evening they **talk shop** all the time!

5 **talk about + adjective** = an expression used to emphasize the adjective you are using
Did you see the game last night? **Talk about exciting!** It was fantastic!

speak

6 **to speak up** = to speak more loudly, so that other people can hear
Sorry, but we can't hear you in the back of the room. Can you **speak up**, please?

7 **to speak too soon** = to say something that you quickly see is not true
I'm sure John isn't coming to the party. Oh, I **spoke too soon**. Look! There he is.

8 **to speak + possessive adjective + mind** = to say strongly and directly what you think about something
Look, Tom, I'm going to **speak my mind**, OK? I think you were really rude to Mandy, and you should say sorry.

9 **not be on speaking terms** [with someone] = to not speak to someone because you have had an argument
James and Allie had an argument last night, and now they're **not on speaking terms**.

10 **can't speak a word of + language** = can't say anything in a foreign language
I've been to Mexico many times, but I **can't speak a word of Spanish**!

Unit 4 Friends

1 **an old friend** = someone who has been a friend for a long time
Jim and I are **old friends**. I've known him since I was four!

2 **a close friend** = a friend who you know very well and really trust
Belinda knows all my secrets! She's a really **close friend**.

3 **to make friends** = to start a friendship
Joanna's very sociable and finds it very easy **to make** new **friends**.

4 **That's what friends are for** = you can say this to a friend who thanks you for doing something special for him or her
"Thanks so much, Jenny. You really helped me." "No problem, Mike – **that's what friends are for.**"

5 **to hit it off** [with someone] = to like someone and become friendly immediately
Alex and I **hit it off** when we met, and now we're really good friends.

6 **friendly advice** = an opinion you give a friend
"Jake, don't get mad at me. I want to give you some **friendly advice**. You should apologize to Doug."

7 **an ally** = a country or person who helps you in a war or time of difficulty
The U.S., France and Britain were **allies** in World War II.

8 **an acquaintance** = someone you know but who is not really a friend
He's not really my dad's friend, he's just **an acquaintance** from work.

Unit 6 Verb + preposition combinations: *with/for/about*

1 I **had fun with** my friends yesterday. We watched some DVDs and played some computer games.

2 I like to **chat with** my friends after school. We just talk about little things, nothing important, but it's nice!

3 My parents don't like some of the people I **hang out with**.

4 That yellow shirt's very nice, but it doesn't really **go with** green pants.

5 Everything on the menu looks great, but I think I'll **go for** the spaghetti.

6 If you don't know the answer, why don't you **search for** it online?

7 My sister's just graduated from college, and now she's **applying for** jobs with a lot of different companies.

8 My dog's really sick. The vet says we can only **hope for** the best, but we think he may not live very long.

9 I don't like being with John. After the first five minutes together, we don't have anything to **talk about**.

10 I just don't think it's funny. There's nothing to **laugh about**!

11 He used to **dream about** being rich. Then he won the lottery, and now he is rich!

12 Look, I think one thing and you don't agree, but we don't need to **argue about** it, do we?

Unit 7 Extreme adjectives

1 The food at that restaurant is really **delicious**. = It tastes very good.

4 We went to a rock concert, and the music was **deafening**! = It was very loud.

7 There was a **terrible** accident last week. Three people were killed. = It was very bad.

2 I couldn't eat the food. It was **disgusting**. = It tasted very bad.

5 We watched a **fascinating** show about whales. = It was very interesting.

8 I went bungee jumping yesterday. I was **terrified**! = I was very frightened.

3 We watched a comedy show last night. It was **hilarious**! = It was very funny.

6 We were **delighted** when we heard your good news. = We were very happy.

9 At the end of the race, I was **thrilled** because I won! = I was very excited.

Unit 8 Expressions with *make*

1 **to make a request** = to ask (for) something
John, can I **make a request**? Can we start the meeting at 10 a.m. and not 9 a.m?

2 **to make an offer** = to say that you will do something or that you will pay a price
I didn't really want to sell my bike, but Rafael **made** me **an offer** of $150, so I took it.

3 **to make a fresh start** = an opportunity to begin something again
The meeting didn't go well this morning, so let's **make a fresh start** this afternoon.

4 **to make a living** = to earn money that you use to buy food, clothes, etc.
She doesn't like her job at all. It's just a way for her to **make a living**.

5 **to make time** = to find space in a day to do something
I'm really busy tomorrow, but I'll try to **make time** to call you, OK?

6 **to make sure** = to take action to be certain that something happens, is true, etc.
I think I locked the door, but I'll go back to the house to **make sure**.

7 **to make room (for)** = to leave space for something, so that it can fit
Our new television is really big! We had to take the sofa out of the living room to **make room** for it!

8 **to make way (for)** = to be replaced by something, especially because it is better, cheaper, easier, etc.
They knocked down six stores on that street to **make way** for a new supermarket.

Unit 9 Noun suffixes: *-ity/-ment/-ness/-ion/-ation*

1 **probability** [adjective: *probable*]
Thomas loves movies, so in all **probability** he's watching one right now.

2 **creativity** [adjective: *creative*]
Writers need a lot of **creativity**. They have to imagine people and places, and tell a good story.

3 **amusement** [verb: *amuse*]
I came in last in the race to my brother's **amusement**. He thought it was really funny.

4 **treatment** [verb: *treat*]
She gets special **treatment** from the teachers because she's so good at sports. It's not fair!

5 **punishment** [verb: *punish*]
I came home really late last night, so my parents say I can't go out for a week as a **punishment**.

6 **advertisement** [verb: *advertise*]
I bought this camera because I saw an **advertisement** for it in a magazine.

7 **madness** [adjective: *mad*]
It's raining, and you're going out for a walk? That's complete **madness**!

8 **blindness** [adjective: *blind*]
Some people have problems with their eyes, and if they don't get medical help, it can result in **blindness**.

9 **action** [verb: *act*]
We can't just sit here and talk about the problem. We need to take **action**!

10 **suggestion** [verb: *suggest*]
So, what are we going to do? Does anyone have a **suggestion**?

11 **expectations** [verb: *expect*]
People have very high **expectations** of the new president. Let's hope she does a good job!

12 **invitation** [verb: *invite*]
Sorry, you can't come in. The party is **invitation** only, and you're not on the guest list.

Unit 10 Crime

Verb		The crime	The criminal
1	to murder = to kill someone intentionally	murder	a murderer
2	to assassinate = to kill someone famous or important	assassination	an assassin
3	to steal = to take something from another person	theft	a thief
4	to mug = to attack someone and take their money or possessions	mugging	a mugger
5	to break in = to get into a building illegally, usually by damaging a window or door	a break-in	

mugger

thief

1 He went to prison for thirty years for **murder**.
He was a terrible man. He **murdered** six people.

2 After shooting the king, the **assassin** managed to escape.
Police have discovered a plot to **assassinate** the president.

3 They were so poor that they had to **steal** money to buy food.
Thieves escaped last night with over $50,000 from the new post office.

4 A friend of mine **was mugged** in town last night. They stole his cell phone and a credit card.
A lot of **muggers** are trying to take money from other people in this city.

5 Someone **broke into** my grandmother's house last week. They smashed a window to get in.
A **break-in** is always upsetting. Having someone get into your home is horrible.

Unit 11 Problems

1 **to cause a problem/problems** = to make a problem happen
Look, I'm sorry. I don't want to **cause** you any **problems**.

2 **to deal with a problem/problems** = to take action to try to solve a problem
How are we going to **deal with** this **problem**?

3 **to run into a problem/problems** = to begin to experience a problem
At first the trip was easy, but then they **ran into** a few **problems**, especially when the weather got bad.

4 **to overcome a problem/problems** = to find an answer to a problem
We had a few **problems**, but we **overcame** them easily.

5 **a problem child** = a child who causes problems
He's always in trouble at school. He's the **problem child** of the family.

6 **a potential problem** = a problem that might happen in the future
So far, everything's OK, but we have one or two **potential problems**.

7 **a major problem** = a very big problem
I have **a major problem**. My computer crashed, and my report is due tomorrow.

8 **a drawback** = a disadvantage or negative part of a situation
I plan to go to Canada. The one **drawback** is that it will cost a lot of money!

9 **a headache** = something that gives you a problem or makes you worry
My computer keeps crashing. It's a real **headache** because I have a lot of work to do!

Unit 12 Phrasal verbs: *up/into/down*

1 **to give something up** = to stop something that is a habit for you
My mom used to eat unhealthy food, but she **gave up** fried food last year.

2 **to put someone up** = to give someone a place to stay
When you come to Lima, we can **put you up** at our house.

3 **to turn up** = to appear, to happen
I couldn't find my camera for days, but it **turned up** in my brother's bedroom!

4 **to look someone up** = to visit or contact someone
Goodbye. If you ever come to Japan, please **look me up**.

5 **to look into something** = to investigate
There's a smell of gas in the kitchen. I think we should **look into it**.

6 **to turn into something** = to become something or someone different
It was a really scary movie, especially when that man **turned into a monster**!

7 **to run into someone** = to meet by chance, accidentally
When I was in town yesterday, I **ran into an old friend** from my high school.

8 **to go into something** = to talk about
It's very personal, so can we please not **go into it**?

9 **to turn something/someone down** = to say "no" to an offer or a request
They offered him a job, but the money wasn't good enough, so he **turned it down**.

10 **to break down** = to stop working, especially a car/bus/motorcycle, etc.
My dad's car **broke down**, so we had to push it!

11 **to get someone down** = to make someone unhappy or depressed
I've been sick for two weeks now. It's beginning to **get me down**.

12 **to put someone down** = to make someone feel unimportant by criticizing them
Why did you **put me down** like that in front of all those other people? I feel stupid now!

Unit 14 Anger

1 **mad** = angry
Jo was **mad** at me when I forgot her birthday.

2 **irritated** = annoyed; a little bit angry
He was asking a lot of silly questions, and I started to get **irritated**.

3 **upset** = unhappy and angry
He was pretty **upset** when you didn't call him back.

4 **indignant** = angry because of something that is unfair or wrong
When I said I thought he was wrong, he got pretty **indignant**.

5 **outraged** = very angry
A lot of people were **outraged** when the government closed the local hospital.

6 **bitter** = angry and unhappy because of bad things that happened in the past
My grandfather didn't let my dad go to college, and Dad's still **bitter** about it.

7 **in a bad mood** = feeling angry and ready to argue
Don't go anywhere near Ned today. He's **in a bad mood**.

8 **to look at someone the wrong way** = to look at someone in an unpleasant way
What's his problem? He **looked at me the wrong way**, and I want to know what's going on.

9 **a heated argument** = an argument where people get angry and excited
They had a really **heated argument** about which soccer team was the best.

Unit 15 Adjectives with negative prefixes

1 **illiterate** = not able to read or write
Some people in the world are **illiterate**. They don't go to school, so don't learn to read and write.

2 **immature** = not behaving in a way expected of someone your age
What? You're crying because I shouted at you? That's really **immature**, Jake.

3 **impersonal** = with little or no human warmth or interest
I don't like hospitals becaues they're very **impersonal** places.

4 **improbable** = not likely to happen or to be true
Most scientists agree that it's highly **improbable** that the Loch Ness Monster exists.

5 **inaccurate** = not correct
That figure is **inaccurate**. There are more than 5 billion people in the world.

6 **inadequate** = not good enough, or too small in quantity
I'm sorry, but your work is **inadequate**, and you'll have to do it again.

7 **incomplete** = not complete, not finished
The new school building is still **incomplete**. It'll be ready next year.

8 **insincere** = not really meaning what you say
When I won, he said, "Good job," but I think he was being **insincere**.

9 **irrational** = not using clear thinking or reason
I know it's **irrational**, but I'm scared of spiders.

10 **unable** = not able to do something
Thank you for calling. We are **unable** to answer your call. Please leave a message.

11 **unattractive** = not good to look at
I think it's a very **unattractive** city. The buildings are all modern and very ugly.

12 **uncertain** = not knowing what to do, not able to decide
I'm **uncertain** about whether to go to college or not. Maybe I'll get a job instead.

Unit 16 Expressions with *feel*

1 **to feel bad/awful about something** = to feel shame or regret for doing or saying something
I said something horrible to my friend Sally, and now I **feel awful about it**.

2 **to feel at home** = to be very relaxed and comfortable, as if you were in your own home
The hotel was very comfortable, and the owner was very kind. We really **felt at home**.

3 **to feel free** = do something without having to ask permission first
If you're hungry, **feel free** to take some food from the fridge, OK?

4 **not to feel a thing** = not feel any pain
The dentist took my tooth out, and surprisingly, I **didn't feel a thing**.

5 **to feel out of place** = to feel uncomfortable somewhere, like you don't belong
Everyone at the party knew all the other people, but I didn't! I really **felt out of place**.

6 **to feel under the weather** = not to feel very well, to feel a little sick
I'm not really sick you know, I just **feel** a bit **under the weather**.

7 **to feel your way** = to use your hands to know where you're going
The room was so dark that I had to **feel my way** along the wall to find the door.

8 **to get the feel of something** = to begin to learn how to do something new
It looks difficult to play this game, but it's easy when you **get the feel of it**.

Grammar reference

Unit 3

Simple past vs. present perfect

1   We use the simple past to talk about complete events which are finished, or before "now," the moment of speaking.
*I **called** you yesterday. Where **were** you?*
*We **didn't have** computers when I **was** born.*

2   We use the present perfect to connect the past and "now," the moment of speaking.
*We've **called** you three times today. Where **have** you **been**?*
*We've **lived** in the same house all our lives.*

3   Use the simple past with *minutes ago, yesterday, last week, when I was ...,* etc.
We often use *for, since, just, already, yet, ever* and *never* with the present perfect.

*They **went** out a few **minutes ago**.*	*They've **just left**.*
*I **saw** that movie **yesterday**.*	*I've **already seen** that movie.*
*I **met** her boyfriend **last weekend**.*	*I've **never met** your girlfriend.*
*We **moved** there **when I was young**.*	*We've **lived** there **since I was a child**.*

Time expressions

1   We use *just* before the past participle to say that something happened a short time ago.
*We've **just arrived**.*   *They've **just gone** out.*

2   We use *already* at the end of the sentence or before the past participle to express surprise or emphasize that something happened.
*Have you **finished already**?*   *We've **already seen** this movie.*

3   We use *yet* at the end of negative sentences to emphasize that something didn't happen (but probably will in the future) and at the end of questions.
*I **haven't started** this exercise **yet**. (but I will)*   *Have you **met** my new boyfriend **yet**?*

4   We use *still* before *hasn't/haven't* in negative sentences, or before *not* in questions, to show surprise that something you expected to happen didn't happen.
*I can't believe you **still haven't said** sorry.*   *Has she **still not told** you the truth?*

Unit 4

Simple past vs. past continuous

1   We use the simple past to talk about actions that happened at one moment in time in the past. We use the past continuous to describe the background actions in progress around that time in the past.

*I **was playing** soccer. (background)*	*I **broke** my leg. (action)*
*We **were having** a picnic. (background)*	*It **started** to rain. (action)*
*What **were** you **doing**? (background)*	*I **called** you. (action)*

2   It is common to use *when* with the simple past to introduce the past action or *while* with the past continuous to introduce the background.
*I broke my leg **while** I **was playing** football.*
*We were having a picnic **when** it **started** to rain.*
*What were you doing **when** I **called** you?*

Time conjunctions: *as / as soon as*

Another expression that we use with the simple past is *as soon as*. We can also use *as* with the same meaning as *while*.
***As soon as** I got home, I turned on the TV for the big game.*
*Someone scored **as** I **was making** a sandwich.*

Simple past vs. past perfect

1   We use the simple past to talk about an event that happened at a specific time in the past.
We use the past perfect when we need to emphasize that one event happened <u>before</u> another.
*The game **had started** when we **got** there.*
*When I **got** to the street I **realized** I **hadn't brought** his address with me.*

*How long **had** you **been** there when they finally **arrived**?*

2   Sometimes it is necessary to use the past perfect to make the meaning clear.
*She'**d left** when I got there. (I didn't see her.)*
*She **left** when I got there. (but I saw her)*

3   It is not necessary to use the past perfect when *before* or *after* is used.
*She left **before** I got there.*

Unit 5

Present perfect vs. present perfect continuous

1   We use the present perfect to emphasize the result or completion of an activity.
*I'**ve copied** that CD you asked me for. Here it is.*
*I'**ve bought** everybody's presents. I'm so organized!*

We use the present perfect continuous to emphasize the activity, not the result or completion of the activity (it may not be finished).
*I'**ve been copying** CDs all morning. I have 10 more to go!*
*I'**ve been shopping** for presents. I still haven't found anything for my sister.*

2   We use the present perfect to emphasize "how many."
*I'**ve written** 10 emails this morning.*   *You'**ve had** three pieces of cake already!*
*How many sandwiches **have** you **made**?*

We use the present perfect continuous to emphasize "how long."
*I'**ve been writing** emails for hours.*   *You'**ve been eating** cake since you got here!*
*How long **have** you **been making** sandwiches?*

had better / should / ought to

We use *should* or *ought to* to give advice or say what we think is a good (or bad) idea. They have the same meaning. Remember, *should* is a modal verb and is used without *to*. We use *had better* to give stronger advice or warnings. The form is always past (never *have better*), but the meaning is present. *Had better* is also used without *to*.
*You **should** take a break.*   *You **shouldn't** worry so much.*
*She **ought to** be more careful.*   *She **ought not to** be so pessimistic.*
*He'**d better** start doing some work.*   *He'**d better not** come near me.*

Unit 6

Future predictions

100% probability	*will*	
↑	*will probably*	*is likely*
	might	*might not*
↓	*probably won't*	*isn't likely to*
0% probability	*won't*	

When we make predictions about the future, we can use *will*, *might* and *be likely to* (and their negative forms) to show how sure we are about the chances of something happening.
*My parents **will be** really angry when I get home tonight. (100% sure)*
*My father **will probably shout** / **is likely to shout** at me.*
*They **might not let** me **go out** again next weekend.*
*My brother **probably won't help** / **isn't likely to help** me.*
*But next weekend, my parents **won't remember** what happened!*

First conditional with *if* and *unless*

In first conditional sentences:

a   both verbs refer to actions or events in the future;
b   the verb tense after the words *if* or *unless* is simple present;
c   the verb tense in the other clause is *will* or *won't*;
d   we can use *if* or *unless* (which means if not);
e   when we use *unless*, the verb that follows is in the affirmative.
*If my friends **visit** me (tomorrow), we'**ll go** out for lunch.*

I'll take them to the Chinese restaurant unless they want to eat pizza. (= .... if they don't want to eat pizza.)
Unless my parents give me some money, I won't be able to pay. (= If my parents don't give ...)

Unit 7

make / let / be allowed to

1   We use *make [someone do]* to talk about an obligation.
    Our teacher makes us do a lot of homework. (= We cannot choose; it's an obligation that our teacher gives us.)
    My older brother made me lend him some money. (= I could not choose; my brother forced me.)

2   We use *let [someone do]* to talk about permission.
    Our teacher lets us leave early on Fridays. (= The teacher gives us permission to leave early.)
    My father let me use the car yesterday. (= My father gave me permission to use the car.)

3   We use *be allowed to [do something]* to say that someone has (or doesn't have) permission.
    At our school, we're allowed to wear jeans if we want to. (= we can wear jeans, but we don't have to)
    When we were young, we weren't allowed to play outside in the street. (= we couldn't play in the street)

Modals of obligation, prohibition and permission

1   *have to / don't have to* is used to talk about obligation / no obligation.
    We don't have to wear a school uniform. (= Wearing a school uniform is not an obligation for us.)
    We didn't have to pay for the meal. (= It was not necessary to pay.)

2   *can / can't* is used to talk about permission.
    You can watch TV if you want to. (= I give you permission to watch TV.)
    We can't go in because we're not 18. (= We don't have permission to go in.)

3   We use *must not* to prohibit someone from doing something or to say that something is very important.
    We must not be late! (= It is very important for us not to be late.)
    You must not talk to me like that! (= I am telling you that I don't allow this.)

Unit 8

Present and past passive review

We form the passive with a form of the verb *to be* + the past participle of the main verb.
English is spoken all over the world.   *My bike was stolen last night.*

Causative have (have something done)

We use *have something done* when we talk about a service or function that someone else does for us.
I had my hair cut last week. (= I went to a hair salon, and a person cut my hair.)
We had our car repaired. (= We've taken our car to a garage, and someone has repaired it for us.)

Present perfect passive

We form the present perfect passive with *have/has been* + past participle.
Our old house isn't there any more. It's been torn down.
The rules of tennis haven't been changed for a long time.

Future passive

We form the future passive with *will be / won't be* + past participle.
Those trees will be cut down next month.
If you don't behave nicely, you won't be invited again!

Unit 9

Gerunds and infinitives

1   When a verb is followed by another verb, the second verb is either in the gerund (-*ing*) or infinitive form. The form of the second verb depends on the first verb.

2   Some verbs (e.g., *enjoy, detest, [don't] mind, imagine, feel like, suggest, practice, miss*) are followed by a verb in the gerund form.
*I don't **enjoy living** in the city very much.*   *She doesn't **feel like going** out tonight.*

3   Other verbs (e.g., *hope, promise, ask, learn, expect, decide, afford, offer, choose*) are followed by a verb in the infinitive form.
*We can't **afford to go** on vacation this year.*   *I **promise to pay** you on Monday.*

Verbs with gerunds or infinitives

1   Some verbs (e.g., *remember, stop, try*) can be followed by a second verb in either the gerund or infinitive form. The form of the second verb depends on the meaning of the sentence.
*I **remember going** to my first soccer game with my dad. (= I remember the occasion.)*
*I **remembered to go** to the stadium and buy the tickets. (= I didn't forget to do this.)*
*I **stopped to watch** the news. (= I was doing something, e.g., my homework / talking to my parents, when the news started. I stopped the first activity because I wanted to watch the news.)*
*I **stopped watching** TV and went to bed. (= I was watching TV. I decided not to watch TV, so I turned off the TV and went to bed.)*

2   Some verbs (e.g., *like, love, hate, prefer, begin, start*) can be followed by gerund or infinitive with no difference in meaning.
*We **began to run** when it **started raining**.*   *We **began running** when it **started to rain**.*

Unit 10

Second conditional review

1   When we want to talk about imaginary actions and their consequences, we use the second conditional.

2   The second conditional has two clauses: "*if* + the past tense" to introduce the hypothetical situation and "*would / could / might* + verb" to talk about the imaginary result.
*If I **had** more time, I **would learn** the guitar.*

3   The clauses can be put the other way around. In this case we don't use a comma.
*I **would learn** the guitar if I **had** more time.*

4   Other ways of saying *if* in a second conditional include *what if, suppose, imagine* and *say*.
***What if** you won the lottery? Would you be happy?*
***Suppose** you could live forever. Would you want to?*
***Imagine** you knew your brother was a burglar. Would you tell the police?*
***Say** you could live anywhere. Where would you choose?*

I wish / if only

1   When we want to talk about how we would like our present life to be different, we can use *wish* or *if only* + the simple past.

2   Although we are talking about our present situation, *wish / if only* are followed by the past tense.
*I wish I **didn't have** so much homework.*   *Dave wishes he **had** a girlfriend.*

3   We use *wish / if only* + *could* when we want to talk about having the ability or permission to do something.
*I wish I **could play** the guitar.*   *Sally wishes she **could go** to the party.*

4   With *I wish / If only* and the verb *be*, use *were* for all subjects.
*If only I **were** taller.*
*I wish she **were** here.*

Unit 11

Linkers of contrast: *however / although / even though / despite / in spite of*

1   *Despite* and *in spite of* are followed by a noun or verb in the gerund form.
    Despite *being very rich, he's not happy.*   **In spite of** *his wealth, he's not very happy.*

2   *Although* and *even though* are followed by a clause.
    Although *they played badly, they still won.*
    Even though *he's lived in Paris for three years, he doesn't speak French.*

3   *However* always starts a new sentence and is followed by a comma.
    I don't usually like action movies. **However,** *I really enjoyed Troy.*

Modals of deduction (present)

1   When we are sure something is true, we use *must.*
    She got 20 birthday cards. She **must** *be popular.*

2   When we are sure something is <u>not</u> true, we use *can't.*
    He's failed the driving test five times. He **can't** *be a very good driver.*

3   When we think there is a possibility something is true, we use *might* or *could.*
    They're speaking Spanish, so they **might** *be Mexican.*
    They **could** *be brother and sister. They look a lot alike.*

Unit 12

Modals of deduction (past)

To make a guess about a past situation, we can use the modal verbs *can't, must, might* and *could (not)* with the present perfect.
You were all alone in the house. You **must have been** *really scared.*
I'm not sure how the vase got broken, but it **might have been** *the dog.*
The police believe that the criminal **could have left** *the country.*
It **couldn't have been** *my husband. He was at home with me all last night.*

Indirect questions with *be*

1   After expressions like *I don't understand …, I wonder …, I want to know …* and *I don't know …* we often use question words. However, what comes after the question word is not a question, and does not follow the word order for questions.
    I wonder **why she said that.** (**NOT** *I wonder why* ~~did she say that.~~)
    I don't know **when we'll arrive.** (**NOT** *I don't know when* ~~will we arrive.~~)
    I want to know **where you're going.** (**NOT** *I want to know where* ~~are you going.~~)

2   We can also use an expression such as *Can you tell me …, Do you happen to know …* and *Do you know … .* These phrases are the questions, so what comes after these expressions does not follow the word order for questions.
    Can you tell me **where the bathrooms are?** (**NOT** *Can you tell me where* ~~are the bathrooms?~~)
    Do you happen to know **if he's French?** (**NOT** *Do you happen to know* ~~is he French?~~)
    Do you know **why she left early?** (**NOT** *Do you know why* ~~did she leave early?~~)

Unit 13

Reported speech (review)

In reported speech, we often change the verb that was used in direct speech.

"It's late," he said.	→	*He said it* **was** *late.*
"I've lost my watch," she said.	→	*She said she'd lost her watch.*
"We didn't enjoy our vacation," they said.	→	*They said they* **didn't enjoy** *their vacation.*
"I can't open the door," my sister said.	→	*My sister said she* **couldn't open** *the door.*
"I'll pick you up at eight," she said.	→	*She said she'd pick me up at eight.*

Reported questions

1 When we report yes/no questions, we use *if* (or *whether*) and statement word order.

"Is Quito very big?"	→	*He asked me **if** Quito was big.*
"Do you play chess?"	→	*She asked me **whether** I played chess.*
"Did your father go abroad last year?"	→	*He asked me **if** my father had gone abroad last year.*

2 When we report *wh-* questions (with *who / where / what / how / when*, etc.), we use the same question word and statement word order.

"Who are you talking to?"	→	*He asked me **who** I was talking to.*
"When did you arrive?"	→	*They asked me **when** I had arrived.*
"How much money have you spent?"	→	*She asked me **how much** money I'd spent.*

3 With requests, we use *asked* + person + *to (do)*.

"Please carry this for me, Mike."	→	*She **asked Mike to carry** it for her.*
"Can you open the window please?"	→	*He **asked me to open** the window.*
"Please don't be late!"	→	*The teacher **asked us not to be** late.*

Reporting verbs

We can use many different verbs to report speech. Be careful about the pattern that follows these verbs.

1 Some verbs (e.g., *say, explain*) are followed by *that* + clause.
   *He **said that** the movie was one of the best he'd ever seen.*
   *She **explained that** she couldn't come because she had work to do.*

2 Some verbs (e.g., *offer, refuse, agree*) are followed by the infinitive with *to*.
   *My mother **offered to lend** me some money.*
   *She **refused to tell** me her name.*
   *I **agreed to go** with them.*

3 Some verbs (e.g., *ask, order, invite, tell, persuade*) are followed by an object + infinitive with *to*.
   *My father **asked my sister to help** him choose a present for my mother.*
   *The police officer **ordered them to stop**.*
   *My grandparents **invited me to have** lunch with them.*
   *Our teacher **told us to concentrate** more.*
   *My friends **persuaded me to go** to the concert with them.*

4 Some verbs (e.g., *apologize for, suggest*) are followed by a noun or a gerund.
   *He **apologized for the noise**. He **apologized for making** a noise.*
   *She **suggested a walk**. She **suggested going** for a walk.*

Unit 14

Third conditional

1 We use the third conditional to speculate about how things might have been different in the past.
   The third conditional is formed with *If* + past perfect + *would (not) have* + past participle.
   *If we'**d waited** for you, we **would have missed** the beginning of the movie.*
   (= We <u>didn't</u> wait for you, so we <u>didn't</u> miss the beginning of the movie.)
   *If you **hadn't fallen asleep** in class, the teacher **wouldn't have made** you stay after school.*
   (= You <u>did</u> fall asleep, and the teacher <u>did</u> make you stay after school.)

2 Instead of *would*, we can use *might* (if we are not very sure of the possible result).
   *If we'**d waited** for you, we **might have missed** the beginning of the movie.*

I wish / If only + for past situations

We use *I wish* or *If only* + past perfect to express regret about past actions or events.
*I wish I'**d called** her. (= I <u>didn't</u> call her, and I regret it.)*
*I wish they **hadn't told** you about it. (= They <u>did</u> tell you, and I regret it.)*
*If only I'**d studied** harder. (= I <u>didn't</u> study hard, and I regret it.)*
*If only we **hadn't argued** with them. (= We <u>did</u> argue with them, and I regret it.)*

should / shouldn't have

We use *should / shouldn't have (done)* to criticize past actions.
*You **should've told** me. (= You <u>didn't</u> tell me, and I think that was wrong.)*
*She **shouldn't have broken** my camera. (= She <u>did</u> break my camera, and that was wrong.)*

Unit 15

Non-defining and defining relative clauses

1 We use relative clauses to add information about the subject or object of a sentence.

2 Relative clauses are introduced by words like *that*, *which*, *where*, *who* and *whose*.

We use *that* to refer to things.
*That's the car **that** almost hit me.*

We use *that/who* to refer to people.
*The woman **who/that** served me was Brazilian.*

We use *where* to refer to places.
*These photos were taken in Paris, **where** we went for our vacation last year.*

We use *whose* to refer to possession.
*She's the girl **whose** brother plays the guitar in a band.*

3 Sometimes the information is essential to know what exactly we are talking about. In these cases, we use a defining relative clause, and we don't use a comma.
*My brother **who** lives in Canada is an architect. (= I have more than one brother, but I am talking about the one who lives in Canada.)*

4 Sometimes the information is additional. We don't need it to understand what we are talking about. This is a non-defining relative clause. The extra information is included between commas. (Note: In these sentences we <u>can't</u> use *that*.) For example:
*My brother, **who lives in Canada**, is an architect. (= I only have one brother. He lives in Canada and is an architect.)*

Definite, indefinite and no article

1 We use the definite article (*the*):

   a when something is unique: *Have you seen **the** moon tonight? It's beautiful.*

   b to talk about the ability to play an instrument: *She plays **the** violin really well.*

   c to refer to specific things: *I love **the** sound of birds singing in the morning.*

   d when we know what is being talked about: *Do you have **the** money? (I lent you last week.)*

2 We use the indefinite article (*a/an*):

   a to talk about professions: *My dad's **a** teacher.*

   b to talk about one thing: *I read **a** really good book last week.*

3 We use no article:

   a to refer to things in general: ***Music** always makes me feel happy.*

   b to talk about places as institutions: *I go to **college** in Los Angeles.*

Unit 16

be used to

1 When we want to say that we are accustomed or not accustomed to doing things, we can use the expressions *be used to* and *get used to*. These expressions are followed by a noun or the gerund (*-ing*) form of a verb.
*He's not used to **being** so popular.*   *She's not really used to young **children**.*

2 *be used to* refers to a state.
*I'm not **used to working** so hard.*

3 *get used to* refers to a process.
*It took me years **to get used to driving** on the left.*

4 Don't confuse these expressions with *used to*, which refers to past habits and is followed by an infinitive without *to*.
*We **used to spend** our summers in Brazil when I was a child.*

Phrasal verbs

1 Phrasal verbs have two or three parts.
*Guess who I **bumped into** yesterday? (met by chance)*
*I really **look up to** my math teacher. (respect)*

2   With some phrasal verbs, these parts can be separated by the object of the verb.
    I **looked up** the word in the dictionary.   OR
    I **looked** the word **up** in the dictionary.

    However, when the object is a pronoun, it must come between the two parts.
    I looked it up. (**NOT** ~~I looked up it.~~)

3   In other phrasal verbs, these parts can never be separated.
    I **take after** my mother. (**NOT** ~~I take my mother after.~~)

4   Three-part phrasal verbs cannot be separated.
    I've **made up with** my girlfriend.

5   To find out if a phrasal verb can be separated or not, look in a dictionary:
    If it **can** be separated, it will be listed: look <u>something</u> up
    If it **can't** be separated, it will be listed: take after <u>somebody</u>

6   Some phrasal verbs have more than one meaning.
    My car's **broken down**. (stopped working)
    When she heard the news, she **broke down**. (started crying)

Notes

Notes

Notes

Notes

Notes

Notes

Thanks and acknowledgments

The authors would like to thank a number of people whose support has proved invaluable during the planning, writing and production process of *American English in Mind*.

First of all we would like to thank the numerous teachers and students in many countries of the world who have used the first edition of *English in Mind*. Their enthusiasm for the course, and the detailed feedback and valuable suggestions we got from many of them were an important source of inspiration and guidance for us in developing the concept and in the creation of *American English in Mind*.

In particular, the authors and publishers would like to thank the following teachers who gave up their valuable time for classroom observations, interviews and focus groups:

Brazil
Warren Cragg (ASAP Idiomas); Angela Pinheiro da Cruz (Colégio São Bento; Carpe Diem); Ana Paula Vedovato Maestrello (Colégio Beatíssima Virgem Maria); Natália Mantovanelli Fontana (Lord's Idiomas); Renata Condi de Souza (Colégio Rio Branco, Higienópolis Branch); Alexandra Arruda Cardoso de Almeida (Colégio Guilherme Dumont Villares / Colégio Emilie de Villeneuve); Gisele Siqueira (Speak Up); Ana Karina Giusti Mantovani (Idéia Escolas de Línguas); Maria Virgínia G. B. de Lebron (UFTM / private lessons); Marina Piccinato (Speak Up); Patrícia Nero (Cultura Inglesa / Vila Mariana); Graziela Barroso (Associação Alumni); Francisco Carlos Peinado (Wording); Maria Lúcia Sciamarelli (Colégio Divina Providencia / Jundiaí); Deborah Hallal Jorge (Nice Time Language Center); Lilian Itzicovitch Leventhal (Colégio I. L. Peretz); Dulcinéia Ferreira (One Way Línguas); and Priscila Prieto and Carolina Cruz Marques (Seven Idiomas).

Colombia
Luz Amparo Chacón (Gimnasio Los Monjes); Mayra Barrera; Diana de la Pava (Colegio de la Presentación Las Ferias); Edgar Ardila (Col. Mayor José Celestino Mutis); Sandra Cavanzo B. (Liceo Campo David); Claudia Susana Contreras and Luz Marína Zuluaga (Colegio Anglo Americano); Celina Roldán and Angel Torres (Liceo Cervantes del Norte); Nelson Navarro; Maritza Ruiz Martín; Francisco Mejía, and Adriana Villalba (Colegio Calasanz).

Ecuador
Paul Viteri (Colegio Andino, Quito); William E. Yugsan (Golden Gate Academy – Quito); Irene Costales (Unidad Educativa Cardinal Spellman Femenino); Vinicio Sanchez and Sandra Milena Rodríguez (Colegio Santo Domingo de Guzmán); Sandra Rigazio and María Elena Moncayo (Unidad Educativa Tomás Moro, Quito); Jenny Alexandra Jara Recalde and Estanislao Javier Pauta (COTAC, Quito); Verónica Landázuri and Marisela Madrid (Unidad Educativa "San Francisco de Sales"); Oswaldo Gonzalez and Monica Tamayo (Angel Polibio Chaves School, Quito); Rosario Llerena and Tania Abad (Isaac Newton, Quito); María Fernanda Mármol Mazzini and Luis Armijos (Unidad Educativa Letort, Quito); and Diego Bastidas and Gonzalo Estrella (Colegio Gonzaga, Quito).

Mexico
Connie Alvarez (Colegio Makarenko); Julieta Zelinski (Colegio Williams); Patricia Avila (Liceo Ibero Mexicano); Patricia Cervantes de Brofft (Colegio Frances del Pedregal); Alicia Sotelo (Colegio Simon Bolivar); Patricia Lopez (Instituto Mexico, A.C.); Maria Eugenia Fernandez Castro (Instituto Oriente Arboledas); Lilian Ariadne Lozano Bustos (Universidad Tecmilenio); Maria del Consuelo Contreras Estrada (Liceo Albert Einstein); Alfonso Rene Pelayo Garcia (Colegio Tomas Alva Edison); Ana Pilar Gonzalez (Instituto Felix de Jesus Rougier); and Blanca Kreutter (Instituto Simon Bolivar).

Our heartfelt thanks go to the *American English in Mind* team for their cooperative spirit, their many excellent suggestions and their dedication, which have been characteristic of the entire editorial process: Paul Phillips, Amy E. Hawley, Jennifer Pardilla, Kelley Perrella, Eric Zuarino, Pam Harris, Kate Powers, Shireen Madon, Brigit Dermott, Kate Spencer, Heather McCarron, Keaton Babb, Roderick Gammon, Hugo Loyola, Howard Siegelman, Colleen Schumacher, Margaret Brooks, Kathryn O'Dell, Genevieve Kocienda, Eliza Jensen, Lisa Hutchins, and Lynne Robertson.

We would also like to thank the teams of educational consultants, representatives and managers working for Cambridge University Press in various countries around the world. Space does not allow us to mention them all by name here, but we are extremely grateful for their support and their commitment.

In Student's Book 2, thanks go to David Crystal for the interview in Unit 9, and to Jon Turner for giving us the idea of using the story of Ulises de la Cruz in Unit 15.

Thanks to the team at Pentacor Big for giving the book its design; the staff at CityVox for the audio recordings; and Lightning Pictures and Mannic Media for the video.

Last but not least, we would like to thank our partners, Mares and Adriana, for their support.

The publishers are grateful to the following illustrators:

Anna Lazareva (Lemonade), David Haughey (3 In A Box), Graham Kennedy, Mark Reihill (Lemonade), Mark Watkinson (Illustration), Rob McClurken, Rosa Dodd (NB Illustration), Tracey Knight (Lemonade)

The publishers are grateful to the following for permission to reproduce copyright photographs and material:

Key: l = left, c = center, r = right, t = top, b = bottom, u = upper, lo = lower, f = far

Photo Credits
Alamy/©GFC Collection p 17 (l), Getty Images/ The Bridgeman Art Library/Nigerian p 17 (r), /The Image Bank/DreamPictures p 28 (8), /The Image Bank/David Trood p 83, /Taxi/Biddiboo p 28 (7), /Taxi/Judith Haeusler p 2; The Kobal Collection/ DANJAQ/EON/UA/Keith Hamshere p 51, /New Line p 54 (D), / Paramount p 54 (A), /20th Century Fox/Merrick Morton p 78, 7 /Universal p 54 (B, C), Photolibrary.com/Cultura/Bill Holden p 28 (1), /Kablonk p 28 (2), /Pixland p 28 (3), /Stockbroker/ Monkey Business Images Ltd p 28 (5), /White p 28 (6); Press Association/AP Photo/World Wide Fund For Nature p 65; /L.J. van Houten p 41, Barbara Lindberg p 34 (t); Shutterstock Images/ Diego Cervo p 48, /Alexia Kruscheva p 15, /privilege p 10, /Gary Yim p 68.

Getty Images/©Kaz Chiba/Photodisc p 8 (t), Getty Images/ ©Photo by Syamsul Bahri Muhammad p 26 (cl), Landov/©Greg Gayne/CBS p 42 (t), Landov/©Sonja Flemming/CBS (b), Alamy/©Martin Shields p 60 (t), AP Images/©Photo by NBCU Photo Bank NBC via AP Images p 66 (cl), agefotostock/©Anette Götz p 84 (cl), Getty Images/©Photo by John Kobal Foundation p 90 (t)